JOURNEYS FROM WIMBLEDON COMMON

To Peter –

enjoy your future
travels as much
as I enjoyed
These!

Neil

ISBN 978-1-909121-00-3

PALACE PARK
PRESS
www.acornindependentpress.com

To Helen, with love

JOURNEYS FROM WIMBLEDON COMMON

Travels inspired by the Wombles

NEIL MATTHEWS

THANKS TO:

Dea Birkett and Jonathan Lorie for encouragement and feedback.

Rory Maclean, Tim Moore and Chris Stewart for professional generosity in sharing their experiences of the writer's life.

Hilary Bradt, Dan Linstead, Brian Page, Adrian Phillips and John Stevenage for their insights into editing and publishing.

Michael Fishwick for saying he'd never heard anything like it.

Rob Penn for saying he would be the first to buy a copy.

Zerina and her children for acting as a Wombles focus group.

Cathie, Mike, Lee-Anne, Keith and the rest of the proofreading team.

Helen, without whom I couldn't have started this book, let alone completed it, for reasons too numerous to mention (including the photos).

My mother for general encouragement.

Jurriaan van Santvoort for information on the history of duelling.

Kate Robertson for her assistance.

Everyone featured in this book (names may have been changed).

The companies who helped to get me there and back.

The extract from 'The Polytechnic Magazine' (ref. UWA/RSP/5/1/18 Vol. XIX July-December 1891) is reproduced by permission of University of Westminster Archive Services.

Respectful acknowledgements to Elisabeth Beresford for creating the Wombles and to everyone who has brought them to print, soundtrack, stage and screen ever since.

CONTENTS

INTRODUCTION

My friend is sitting in the comfortable green leather chair. I squeeze him till he sings. His hat is jammed on his head and his scarf is wound round his neck, as if he is about to brave the elements of an English summer day. He won't do that. He has developed a reputation for not doing much at all. That doesn't matter. I first saw him over 30 years ago and he is funny and charming today, as he was then. He doesn't say anything. But he will break into song, and wrinkle his snout, if you press his paw. I don't have any other friends who can do that – or any other friends who are named after a South American river.

Orinoco is one of the Wombles who live on Wimbledon Common, picking up 'things that the everyday folks leave behind'. The Wombles came into the world in 1968 (like me), in the first of a series of books by a journalist named Elisabeth Beresford. After the first book featured on the BBC's *Jackanory* series, the Corporation commissioned producer FilmFair to make a series of animated Wombles episodes. Actor Bernard Cribbins supplied the narration and all the voices, Mike Batt wrote the music and lyrics for the theme tune and millions of small children found a new set of furry friends. Each episode brought five minutes of adventure as the Wombles did their bit to keep the world in order.

It seemed like a wonderful world to a small boy in the early 1970s. My older brother had left home at the earliest opportunity. My older sister showed no interest in the Wombles as far as I can recall. The posters in her bedroom were of Snoopy and Barry Manilow. Years later, she married a man with a prominent nose.

So it was my younger brother and me watching TV while sitting on a black leather sofa, which squeaked the house down if you dared to move a muscle. From time to time, we would run upstairs to the main living room – a vast territory which our parents had attempted to shrink by decorating it in black and importing ever more items of bulky furniture. There was a piano, on which my mother would practise classical compositions. For inspiration, she played recordings of performances by Alfred Brendel. One day, the maestro's rendition of *Für Elise* drifted down the stairs as our grandmother came to visit, leading her to conclude that Mother's practising was beginning to pay off. I would ascend to the heights of piano grade 1 (118 marks out of 150), while my brother would murder various tunes with the aid of a trumpet, in our bedroom at the other end of the first floor.

My father was stationed in the newsagent's shop which he ran at the front of the house, looking out onto Harrow's main street. My brother and I would run into the shop on daily raids for crisps and Opal Fruits, to tell him if England had lost another wicket or to read one of the magazines. At one stage, the shop stocked selections of children's books, enabling me to enjoy the entire Famous Five canon for free. Sometimes my reading would stray into more adult material such as the Sherlock Holmes short stories. But it was never long before I returned to children's literature, much of it from the local library – though not for a while after the discovery under my bed of the library copy of *Noggin the Nog*, four years after it should have been returned.

The term 'hyperactive' didn't apply to my brother or me. We walked to school, but showed little talent for sport, apart from cricket in which I bowled off-spinners so slow that the batsman was out of form by the time the ball reached him. Our lack of outdoor exercise was influenced by a desire to avoid being run over by the never-ending traffic on the high street. The upstairs living room hosted Scalextric competitions, but for the most part our books and the TV were enough.

There was plenty of TV for us to enjoy: the 1970s had a wider range of children's programmes in Britain than ever before. Oliver Postgate was busy narrating the Norse saga of *Noggin the Nog*, the tales of the Moon-based mice known as *The Clangers* and stories of Bagpuss, an old cloth cat who lived in a shop and who – along with various other toys which came to life – would inspect a different lost or broken object in each episode and attempt to deduce its origins. Eric Thompson's gentle voice related *The Magic Roundabout*'s tales of little girl Florence and her friends Dougal the dog, Brian the snail, Dylan the rabbit and Ermintrude the cow.

There was the battle of the magazine format shows, with children defining themselves as *Blue Peter* or *Magpie* fans with all the fervour of sports supporters. Our household watched *Blue Peter*. Despite having no artistic ability, I sat glued to *Vision On* and its examples of other children's artwork which, the presenters told us each week, couldn't be returned. *Doctor Who* (made by the BBC's Drama Department, but loved by children) got a new lease of life with Tom Baker in the title role. Thirty years later, children who had watched him as the Doctor were making TV programmes themselves and hiring Baker as a voiceover artist.

Up against such stiff competition for our attention, the Wombles more than held their own, with their domestic eccentricities, accidents and adventures. They have stood the test; they're as quirky, endearing and funny as ever.

The patriarch of the group is Great Uncle Bulgaria, in his tartan shawl and hat. Bulgaria runs the burrow and it's his initiatives that drive many of the stories – whether instructing Tobermory to repair the telephone system, conducting an impromptu Wombles orchestra or reminiscing about the age of steam. Bulgaria is hard to disconcert, although he does get cranky if the young Wombles don't find him a copy of *The Times* each day. Behind the sternness is a twinkle: he is still sprightly enough to play golf on the common, and mischievous enough to get a cardboard cake baked for the younger Wombles, as a 'Womble Fool's Day' joke.

The resident engineer, Tobermory, makes everything work with ingenuity and imagination. Where Orinoco sees a hammerhead shark, Tobermory knows it is a vacuum cleaner. And when Bulgaria's rocking chair breaks, Tobermory repairs it with a tyre that Orinoco finds on the common. Like Bulgaria, Tobermory has a childlike side to him. After the younger Wombles steal some buttercup crumpets from the kitchen, Tobermory does the same, with the same result – hiccups. For all his inventions, Tobermory is fallible like anyone else. His paper-transporting hotline is a failure, as Madame Cholet does not appreciate the 'borrowing' of her washing line and clothes pegs.

The nearest Womble to Great Uncle Bulgaria in age – or so it seemed to me as a child - is Madame Cholet, the cook with the frilly hat and French accent. She seems to have the classic chef's temperament, too: the kitchen is Madame Cholet's domain, and she is not shy of telling all and sundry to leave. Otherwise she fulfils a traditional female role, cleaning and dusting, or 'rearranging the dust' as the script put it.

Among the young Wombles, Wellington is the class swot; small, shy, bespectacled and with a blue and black school cap. The other young Wombles respect him for his creativity and intelligence. Give Wellington two tins and a long piece of string and, hey presto, he'll give you an inter-Womble communication device. When Tobermory needs help creating a new system for Great Uncle Bulgaria, he enlists Wellington first. And Wellington isn't only a scientist: he can paint – albeit in an abstract fashion which renders Bulgaria in the style of a fried egg. In recent years, my wife Helen has pointed out a disturbing similarity between Wellington and Sven-Göran Eriksson, the phlegmatic Swedish football coach. Maybe it's the glasses.

If Wellington is the intellectual heavyweight of the young Wombles, there is no doubt who provides the muscle: Tomsk. His enthusiasm exceeds his brainpower, and he has a dangerous tendency to take ladders away without checking if anyone is at the top of them. Tobermory's instructions on how to fix the burrow pipeline confuse Tomsk, who mixes up the telephone and water systems, with soggy results. But there's no Womble better for mixing cement or tossing the caber in the Womble Highland Games… even if it does end up in Madame Cholet's vegetable garden. Tomsk does get the occasional *bon mot*: when he sees Bulgaria's head stuck through a painting, he tells the old Womble that 'You've been framed'. But Tomsk's strength is his strength.

Bungo's role, on the other hand, is less obvious. The events of the original book *The Wombles* are seen through his eyes. As the newest and youngest Womble, he is chided by Great Uncle Bulgaria for choosing such a silly name. In the TV episodes, by contrast, Bungo isn't the most intelligent, or the strongest, or even the funniest – although he is inclined to be bossy. He has his heroic moments, such as his rescue of Wellington when a human comes onto the common (possibly the only rescue in literature by a character disguised by a cardboard box). For the most part, though, Bungo is just one of the gang.

The most popular Womble with my brother, my friends and me was Orinoco. He is fat and lazy and is obsessed with food and sleep, or 'forty winks' as he calls it. In one story, when Madame Cholet makes a picnic for the younger Wombles, Orinoco asks for cake, biscuits, buns, a big cake, lemonade, some biscuits and cake, and some sandwiches, and some cake. Bungo and Tomsk join him for the picnic, and Orinoco lightens the picnic hamper... by eating the lot. He is sensitive about his weight, and sometimes tries to do something about it. When Tobermory starts to convert an old grandfather clock into a weighing machine, Orinoco embarks on a frantic sequence of walks and press-ups... only to find that he now weighs ten past three. Much of the comic relief is at his expense. It is Orinoco who is scared by Great Uncle Bulgaria's ghost stories, and hit by randomly flying objects – though this may be a consequence of Orinoco's frequent naps.

Other Wombles share the burrow with this magnificent seven. Miss Adelaide looks after the Womblegarten, and can bring the most unruly young Womble to attention, or for that matter the older ones, including Great Uncle Bulgaria. Younger Wombles include Alderney, Shansi and – in the 1990s version of the TV programme – Stepney. At various points in the books and TV programmes, we meet Wombles from round the world, but that world revolves around Wimbledon.

The Wombles of Wimbledon Common are a family, if an unconventional one – in contrast with the worlds of Charlie Brown or Tom and Jerry, where adults are rare. They live in a world with many attractions for a little boy. Nobody has to go to school and nobody gets hurt – although, unlike their near-namesakes the Weebles, Wombles do fall down – quite a lot, as it happens.

The scripts address their young audience without patronising them. One episode introduces the subject of multiplication and calculating machines while, in another, Wellington asks Tobermory to 'elucidate' on his ideas.

The Wombles have tasted the high life of pop stars. Mike Batt wrote the songs and a number of professional musicians have chosen to dress up, on stage or screen, as fictional furry animals to perform them. The songs gave Batt an excuse to run the gamut of musical genres, from the country and western *Nashville Wombles* through the Beach Boys parody *Non-Stop Wombling Summer Party* to the *Empty Tidy Bag Blues*. Several singles got into the top 20, and the Wombles appeared on *Top of the Pops* on various occasions, exhorting us all to enjoy a *Wombling Merry Christmas* and to join in with the unforgettable *Remember You're a Womble*. Their fame became international; they were the interval act at the Eurovision Song Contest one year. They might have won if they'd been the UK entry.

They weren't content with books, TV series, a film and a musical career. You could buy Wombles-themed clothing, games, household appliances, furnishings and toiletries. There were Wombles toys, including a singing Orinoco. I bought one, and he's sitting in my living room all these years later. It's impossible not to smile when a press of Orinoco's left paw induces a chorus of *Remember you're a Womble* and an outbreak of snout-wrinkling. It isn't obvious why or how a Womble might forget their essential Wombleness. Orinoco and his fellow Wombles are unique and memorable for two reasons.

The first is something which the most prescient writer might not have predicted back in the late 1960s when the first book *The Wombles* was published: the extent to which environmental concerns have come into the centre of our lives. Greenhouse gases and carbon footprints weren't a glint in the eye of mainstream 1970s politics, and global warming had yet to attain the status of having more believers than Father Christmas. The Wombles' burrow, with its doors made of mirrors and walls decorated with old newspapers, gives a homely vision of recycling.

The second is the mechanism for choosing each Womble's name. Up to a certain age, a Womble is nameless. But then they have to sit down with Great Uncle Bulgaria and choose a name from his atlas. This stroke of authorial genius brings the exotic to a reassuring and familiar setting. Some Wombles live over 200 years, with a few reaching the grand old age of 300, so it's just as well there are no Wombles called Constantinople or Leningrad. Imagine having to explain to a six-year-old why they had changed their names to Istanbul Womble and St Petersburg Womble.

I am not a Womble. However, as Orinoco continues to gaze out of the window – dreaming of food or a new concept album – there is something I can do which the Wombles couldn't: visit the places which gave the Wombles their names. For Chairman Mao, a journey of a thousand miles began with a single step. For me, a journey of 50,000 miles begins with a singing Womble.

Does anything connect the places, apart from Wombles? Do the places match up to the Wombles to whom they gave their names? Is Orinoco full of fat, lazy people? Is Cholet stuffed with chefs? Were the Wombles the forerunners of modern environmentalism?

Let's go Wombling and find out – starting where it all began...

WIMBLEDON

I walk out of Wimbledon station, past the ranks of black taxis with drivers stuck in a no-man's-land between alertness and boredom. I cross the road at the traffic lights, stepping around the bollards and barriers indicating roadworks. A passing glance at the car showrooms, pubs and bars, then I start the slow ascent of the deceptive steep hill which bends round to the left, dodging the joggers, and the more dangerous pedestrians with their trolleys on wheels which sway from side to side behind their owners as if on an Olympic slalom course. Bit by bit, the sleepiness induced by the slow trip on the District Line is fading.

Others are about their business, returning laden from shopping trips or nipping into a fashionable bar for a mid-morning drink. My attention focuses on the top of the hill, then the end of the High Street where the war memorial stands.

I pause in silent respect – and to get my breath back – before hurrying off to the left. A large array of white tents is billowing in the gentle breeze. A steady stream of parents is pushing prams, carrying small infants, holding other children by the hand or managing all three feats at once, all heading for the tent. A crowd has gathered by the entrance, around a furry, bespectacled figure.

It can't be easy walking around in a Great Uncle Bulgaria costume. As befits his great wisdom, the head is heavy, which leads to a tendency to nodding, and so is the rest of the outfit. It must have its advantages on winter days – though speed and anonymity are not among them. Today, the oldest Womble of them all is here for publicity purposes; to help with the republication in new editions of Elisabeth Beresford's original Wombles books.

Given the many characters to flit across children's TV screens since the 1970s, I had wondered whether this event would appeal to the children of 2010, or whether it would be a chance for others of my age to relive their youth. Judging from the enthusiasm which Great Uncle Bulgaria's appearance generates, the answer seems to be: both. Nodding his great behatted head in acknowledgement, the old Womble offers one paw to the children swarming round him from every side, while clutching a bent old walking stick for support.

'I know who you are!' shouts one little boy. 'I've *seen* you. I've *seen* you.'

A little girl with a pudding haircut, wearing a pink coat, is hoisted by her mother to Bulgaria's eye level. She doesn't want to speak with him. The little girl is holding her own Womble, whose blue school cap identifies him as Wellington. She waves Wellington's paw as camera phone flashes go off in all directions. At length, after Great Uncle Bulgaria has greeted everyone in turn, we wander into the tents (an eclectic mix of shabby green flooring, DIY store garden chairs, tables with a variety of colouring pens and other equipment and… chandeliers).

'Right, hello, everybody and welcome to this very special event,' intones a short, rotund woman, her long fair hair falling onto the shoulders of her black cardigan. In Womble terms, there's no doubt about it: a bossy nature means she is one of life's Bungos. 'My name is Kate and I'm here to introduce you to the Wombles.'

With the help of cue cards, she mentions some of the best-known Wombles, and one or two who are not so familiar to most people: Cousin Yellowstone, who turns up in the first Wombles book, and Alderney.

'Later on, I'll be reading from the story where Bungo chooses his name. Because all Wombles get their names in a very specific way...'

My mind drifts onto the question of names and naming. Bungo does get a hard time from the older Wombles for his choice of name. But naming yourself, or being named, after a place on an atlas is not that silly a method. In the land of celebrity, stranger by far than a Wombles burrow, the Beckhams named one of their sons after a district of New York in which they conceived him, or where Mrs Beckham found out that she was pregnant: I forget which. The point is that Brooklyn Beckham was lucky. He could have been named Peckham, or Beckenham. It isn't clear whether Paris Hilton gained her name from similar thinking; it's just as possible that she opted for a classier version of her real name, Reading Travelodge. Celebrities may not have the same thought processes as lesser mortals when naming their offspring, particularly rock stars - as Moon Unit Zappa, Zowie Bowie and the Geldof/Yates daughters Fifi Trixiebelle, Tiger Lily Heavenly Hirani and Peaches Honeyblossom have good reason to know. On the other hand, some opportunities have gone begging: it's too late now, but if only Peter Cushing had married Whoopi Goldberg.

The great British public takes a more conservative, but less imaginative, line as a whole. The top ten names for baby boys at present are a laddish trio of Jack, Harry and Alfie, and baby girls tend to receive more delicate names such as Olivia, the retro but rather nice Lily and Sophie. A rose by any other name, whatever Billy Shakespeare says, does not smell as sweet. The children, toddlers and babies fidgeting, giggling, gurgling and running back and forth in the tent will find that their parents' choice of names does make a difference.

Great Uncle Bulgaria and Orinoco

Bungo Kate is exhorting her audience: 'The Wombles help to tidy up after humans because we're often untidy. Now none of you are untidy, are you? Who likes a good tidy up?'

A chorus of enthusiastic assents comes from the children, supplemented by less enthusiastic mumbles from their parents.

'Well, now we're going to do some activities. Who brought odd socks with them? Don't worry if you don't – we have some spares for you to use.'

The odd sock monster, who lurks in washing machines and laundry baskets parting sock pairs and leaving the owners with only one, seems to be as effective as always judging by the forest of hands holding up individual socks.

'If you have your own odd socks, go to the table on the left. If you need an odd sock, go to the table on the right and let's get started!'

The publicity for the launch mentioned 'the chance to make your own Womble'. To this end, the organisers have provided an assortment of socks, glue, buttons, colouring pens and… that's about it. With a number of large adult helping hands, the children get busy. The Womble spirit of tidiness prevails and there is far less mess and distress than, say, at your average airport departure lounge.

The sock puppets which emerge from this mass of young creativity are not, as Bones McCoy would put it, Wombles as we know them. Their eyes are bright and they snake around in camp or menacing fashion (depending on whose hand they are worn on), but they don't have the quirkiness of Wombles. There may be better results once the children and adults have taken the printed instructions home, and tried more of the options suggested, such as pasta for the eyes; peanuts or pasta for the ears; beads, jingle bells, pom-poms or pasta for the nose; and, for an accessorised Womble, upside-down cups for hats or strung beads for necklaces or earrings. If there's a pasta shortage crisis any time soon, you know where to look.

The organisers have other exercises on which the young audience can vent their energies. Drawings of Wombles in their burrows receive a vigorous colouring in. Near-identical pictures of Wombles in hot air balloons invite readers to 'spot the difference'. For the more literate, there's a Womble word search puzzle. For the next Elisabeth (or Olivia or Jack or Harry) Beresford, there's a challenge to write a new Womble story, including a selection of key words. One girl's effort reads:

'It was early in the morning and the sky was a brilliant blue. The wombles were all up trying to find things to recycle. The young wombles were playing among the trees jumping up to catch falling seeds. They soon had to start work though, so they collected some rubbish. They found a ball, a sandwich container and a dog toy by a dustbin. Suddenly, a growl from behind them made them jump, a dog with big sharp teeth made a hiddeous snarl. They ran back to their burrow…'

Apart from the problem with 'hideous', that's impressive from a girl who can't be more than eight years old. It's a great advance on my school days, when a challenge to create a sentence containing the word 'centimetre' produced the result, 'My aunt was coming to the station and I was centimetre.'

I've stayed away from the sock-Womble making, remembering the paucity of my efforts in art at school (a fair assessment would have been 'no talent, darling'). However, one of my companions for the day is getting some attention. While Helen surveys the scene, wondering how she got into this mad endeavour and pining for a visit to one of the local cafés, Orinoco sits on my lap, indifferent to the stares and smiles he is attracting from children and, in some cases, their parents. Six-month-old Minnie removes her thumb from her mouth long enough to make an unsuccessful attempt to remove Orinoco's hat from his head.

Then a girl of no more than six wanders up to my seat and looks deep into Orinoco's eyes. Her mother (black leather coat, practical trousers and whirling digital camera) is more vocal as she hustles up to join us.

'Hello,' she says to Orinoco with a smile, before looking down at her daughter. 'Say hello to Orinoco, darling…'

The girl continues her silent, curious stare. I wave Orinoco's paw at her, to no avail.

'Isn't he sweet?' says the girl's mother.

'Yes, he is,' I reply. 'Try squeezing his paw,' I say to the little girl. She doesn't move.

After a short pause, her mother does the necessary, and jumps as *Remember You're a Womble* blasts out, and Orinoco's snout moves from side to side.

'Oh, my goodness,' says the mother. 'My husband is going to wet himself when he sees this. Stuart! *Stuart!*'

The strains of the song are dying away as her husband arrives, a tall bearded man in his thirties.

'Stuart, it's Orinoco,' explains the mother. 'But this one sings!'

The husband says nothing and tries to look unimpressed, and I wonder why. Then I spot what he's holding: an older and smaller Orinoco who, guessing from the mother's comment, does not sing. Now I understand why the husband doesn't want to reply: it's as obvious a case of Womble envy as you could wish to see.

By now, the event is winding down. The children have made their sock puppets, solved their word searches, written their stories and coloured in their Wombles. They've enjoyed a reading from *The Wombles* of which the most remarkable aspect is Bungo Kate's interpretation of Tobermory's voice as pure Zummerset yokel.

It's time to eat a piece of Womble cake – a sponge decorated with an edible transfer version of one of the Womble book covers – and to pose for some more photos with Great Uncle Bulgaria. One coffee-coloured girl with curly hair clings to Bulgaria's midriff, refusing to let go. The adults wait with practised patience, to take their children away or to pose for a photo themselves. As the tent empties, it's clear that the Wombles have found the favour of a new generation.

* * *

I first visited Wimbledon on one of those late September days when the sun shines and a warm and fuzzy feeling steals over you, and you don't have to be anywhere, at any time, unless you choose.

Wimbledon High Street was glistening in the bright light, a shrine to comfortable middle class prosperity. Jeeves of Belgravia, numerous jewellers and ladies' fashion shops loomed with effortless superiority over my scruffy jeans and faded shirt. Clans of Wimbledonians sat at the pavement cafés, sipping their skinny lattes and admiring their village. For, strange to relate, this part of the world had decided that it should be known as Wimbledon Village. There was no village hall, no blacksmith and no village green where cricket is played or maypoles are danced around. All it had was urban sophistication.

I was visiting Wimbledon Common, birthplace of the Wombles over forty years ago. There are three commons: about 460 hectares of countryside split between Wimbledon Common, Putney Heath and Putney Lower Common (though Putney Lower is separated from the other two). Most of the commons is a Site of Special Scientific Interest and Special Area of Conservation. There is woodland, scrubland, heathland and nine ponds, all of which host bird, animal and plant life. Being unfenced, the whole area is open to the public 24 hours a day throughout the year. There are also golf courses, cricket and rugby pitches, a café, stables, an information centre and a windmill, which is now a museum. That's not counting the cottages dotted around the commons, which house the staff who run the commons.

All life, it seemed, was here, in perfect order. The BMWs, Audis and sports cars sat obediently in a neat and never-ending line. Teenagers in skimpy summer clothes lay face down, skimming their paperback novels or gazing into the distance. Cyclists and joggers passed me as if on an invisible conveyor belt. There was little rubbish: whether this was a result of activities by Wombles or their human trainees was unclear.

In a breach of all known conventions on the matter, I visited the Windmill Tearooms before the windmill itself, for a hot chocolate. The teashop's blackboard was a mine of information, in neat capital letters: 'WINDMILL TEAROOMS: QUESTIONS ANSWERED'.

The blackboard expounded on the role of napkins ('WE KEEP THESE BEHIND THE COUNTER TO AVOID LITTERING OUTSIDE') and pigeons ('HELP US NOT TO ENCOURAGE THEM EATING YOUR LEFTOVERS BY DISPOSING OF YOUR FOOD'). Woe betide the customer who considered asking for Marmite – 'MADE BY THE DEVIL! NEVER!'

At the next table, an Australian family nursed their drinks. They had been to the windmill and its museum and had emerged with their spoils: a Great Uncle Bulgaria toy, clutched by a little girl.

'It's supposed to go with our Australian beanie toy,' explained the mother, showing me a rather generic blue bear with the Australian flag all over its midriff. I introduced them to Orinoco but, for some reason, he wouldn't sing. It served me right for attempting Womble one-upmanship.

The Windmill itself had a two storey octagonal base and a conical tower. It housed a history of windmills, from early Persian and Greek models to modern wind farms. One display wryly noted that the building of new nuclear power stations would be a much more reliable way than wind farms to generate large amounts of electricity, but would 'probably not be popular' in Britain.

A small display was devoted to Lord Baden Powell, who repaired to a small cottage near the windmill in 1908 in order to complete his manuscript of *Scouting for Boys*. The display case contained a note from Baden Powell apologising for not having yet come up with a similar scouting book for use by girls. Still, he wrote, 'many girls have gained much enjoyment from *Scouting for Boys*'. I bet they did.

A large, middle-aged man sat in contemplation, minding the small shop near the Windmill's entrance. I looked round. In among the tat for tourists were… Bungo, Great Uncle Bulgaria and Wellington in a glass case. Like

Orinoco back home, they were 1990s versions of their famous originals. Bulgaria didn't look a day over 300, but the cap sitting, wrong way round, on Bungo's head was a crime against fashion. I bailed him out by buying him, Bulgaria and Wellington. Along with Orinoco, they would be companions for Helen and me on the journeys to come.

After a meander along one of the many paths that crisscross the commons, I sat on a bench to enjoy a bacon and cream cheese bagel. A Labrador smelt the prospect of a snack and sniffed round my ankles. A few minutes later, a small pug did its best to climb onto the bench for its chance of bagel heaven. Neither got what they wanted. On such a day, I didn't begrudge them for trying.

In the sunshine and the breeze, an informal procession unfolded: cyclists, joggers, walkers and families with (mostly) small children and (mostly) smaller dogs. It was almost too perfect. I wondered if I would wake up and find it had all been a dream, or maybe an advertisement for a building society. Then came Ziggy, and the accident.

Ziggy was a spaniel, or mostly spaniel, with patches of brown and cream, floppy ears and a way of running all over the footpath with his paws splayed (not so much a King Charles spaniel as a Charlie Chaplin spaniel). He was some way behind his family – a thickset man in his early forties and two earnest little boys aged around seven and five. They turned towards Ziggy, no doubt for the thousandth time that day.

But this time was different. Racing up behind Ziggy in a blur of testosterone were two large, black-clad men on two large black bikes. Ziggy didn't see them, or heed the father's warning calls, until it was too late. The bikers couldn't brake in time. Ziggy disappeared in a tangle of brown and cream and dirt under the wheels.

Father and sons dashed back, fearing the worst. Before fears could become tears, Ziggy was on his feet again, barking in bewilderment and half-running, half-bouncing, from one side of the path to the other and back. The father got to him, held him down, muttered soothing words in his ears and checked for injuries. There seemed to be none.

The bikers stood to one side for a few minutes, asking after Ziggy; not, I sensed, from great concern, but more out of embarrassment – as if they'd been caught evading their tennis club membership fees. If Wimbledon was a village, I reflected, these were its idiots. Eventually, they remounted their bikes and resumed their race.

'They were going far too fast,' the father explained to the boys. 'There are millions of dogs round here, it was stupid to be cycling that fast...'

Although there might have been some internal bruising, Ziggy seemed healthy enough. Maybe he even enjoyed the attention as a change from trailing behind on a walk. His family put him on a lead and took him home.

***

Wimbledon and its commons used to be less crowded. Medieval Wimbledon could boast nothing more than uncultivated commons and empty roads. The area was once part of the estates of Archbishop of Canterbury. Though William Cecil (16th century secretary of state to Edward VI and later Elizabeth I) leased a house in Wimbledon, his family left in 1639. The local population was in decline by the early 18th century. It took the arrival of the first Earl Spencer, who moved into a new manor house in 1756 – and who took an interest in the area – to create a mini-boom in local employment, through the building of new mansions and then, early in the next century, the building of the main windmill, along with other mills and water wheels for the manufacture of copper utensils.

In the mid-Gregorian period, Wimbledon became the focus of a certain amount of political activity. Prime

Minister William Pitt the Younger often stayed at the house of antislavery campaigner William Wilberforce and Pitt's opponent, Charles James Fox, occupied another local house. The political and military tensions of the time, dominated by the Napoleonic Wars, led Pitt to duel with another opponent, George Tierney, on Putney Heath. In a parliamentary debate in May 1798, Tierney questioned the necessity of haste in the passage of a bill intended for the better manning of the Royal Navy. Pitt replied, 'How can the hon. Gentleman's opposition to it be accounted for, but from a desire to obstruct the defence of the country?' Tierney attacked this comment as unparliamentary, but Pitt would neither apologise nor explain.

The duel, on 27 May, was not fatal to either man. If Tierney had killed the incumbent PM, in wartime, then the verdict of the courts or violent popular opinion would surely have cost him his life in return. There was no advantage in turning Pitt the Younger into Pitt the Posthumous. As it was, Tierney raised his political profile with his fellow Whigs, while Pitt could demonstrate his political stature through standing by his comments in a duel. Honour, as the saying goes, was satisfied.

As late as 1831, the census registered Wimbledon's population as no more than 2,000. The expansion of the railways, with Wimbledon becoming a junction and Waterloo opening in 1848, was the key to the expansion of Wimbledon in turn. Terraced houses began to house increasing numbers of signalmen, dressmakers and blacksmiths, before the professional classes began to move to Wimbledon, as a convenient place from which to commute to their work in London. The population grew to 15,000 by 1881 and then still faster to 55,000 by 1911. Electric trams had arrived by then and, as a reflection of the changing of the social profile of Wimbledon, trams before 7a.m. had to offer a 'workman's fare' of 1d for their journeys.

By now, the British Empire had reached its zenith, with such a brazen level of self-confidence that we could even invite Kaiser Wilhelm II of Germany over to inspect 22,000 troops on Wimbledon Common in July 1891. As one account of the day makes clear, though, it would take more than a German Emperor to interrupt the important events of the social season:

'Saturday last was a gala day at Wimbledon. It was not only that the German Emperor was there in full array – it was not only that the volunteers were there in their thousands – these were no doubt great attractions to many, but to a by no means inconsiderable bevy of fair maidens and their masculine admirers the chief centre of interest at Wimbledon was the Poly fete [the Regent Street Polytechnic, later to become the University of Westminster] at Merton Hall.

'The Cricket and Lawn Tennis Sections of the P.A.C. [Polytechnic Athletics Club] had combined to entertain their lady friends, and they were rewarded by a large attendance, as was indeed to have been expected in a country like England, where manly outdoor games have always been a sure passport to the smiles and favours of the fair sex. The weather was all that could be desired for cricket, the leading summer sport, and also for tennis, an increasingly popular game, a cool breeze wafting pleasantly across the ground keeping players and onlookers in a comfortable condition.

'The decorations, profuse and tasty, put up as a welcome to his august Majesty, lent an additional attraction to the day's proceedings. A programme, neatly put up, set forth the various events, so everything took place in its proper order. The usual fixtures were commenced and during their progress many friends began to arrive, some in couples, others in clans. Entering by the side gate the coup d'oeil was most enchanting. Hard by the First Eleven match, a pretty crowd – in which white dresses, looking cool, seasonable, and in thorough keeping with the fashions of the day, predominated – stood beneath the shady trees, enjoying the game.

'In the distance one could discern the tennis courts, patronised to their utmost capacity, and here and there leisurely strolled the ladies, having their attention well taken up by the flying balls (always so intimate on these occasions) and the recognitions of their athletic friends.

'Shortly after five a move was made by those concerned to the wicket prepared for the Ladies v Gentlemen match, a start at once being made.

'Going to the wicket first, the ladies caused no little amusement to the many spectators (sympathetic and otherwise) by their earnest endeavours to "knock up" a big score. Their wickets fell too rapidly, several of the fellows proving adepts with their left-handed deliveries. A little stand was, however, fortunately made near the close of the innings, and when the last wicket fell thirty runs were registered. Towards these the Misses Saunders, Garrett, Seabrook, and Captain GA Parker chiefly contributed, the remaining batswomen being Mrs Seabrook and Mrs Whittington, and Misses Parker, Longley, Oduim, Price, Tickner, Wilton and Smith. With but twenty minutes left to play, "the male creation", under HL Gambles, commenced with a will, and when time was called the score stood 29, with 5 wickets to spare – a draw in their favour. In fairness to the ladies it is only right to say that they generously allowed their opponents to play lefthanded with ordinary bats, instead of right-handed with broomsticks, the latter proving too fragile for the purpose.

'Cricket over, the general secretary, Charlie Pledger, made the welcome announcement that tea was ready in the marquee erected close by. Needless to say, hearty justice was done to the good things provided. The dessert of strawberries and cherries was received with strong approbation, one table in particular distinguishing itself.

In fact, it put one in mind of children at a Sunday School when the cake is "trotted out". However, it was expressive of the good humour which prevailed, and so the time passed pleasantly away. A raid was afterwards made on the flowers that adorned the tables, and then an adjournment took place to the pavilion, where an excellent concert wiled away the evening time. It was a pretty sight, and must have given great pleasure to the hon. secs. of both sections, as they looked after the "full house," the plentiful light giving a nice effect to the summer costumes. The programme was well arranged, and meritoriously supported by Misses Fergusson, Sharer, Tickner, and Erskine, and Messrs Stanton, Thomson, Johnson, Cockle, and Staples. Mr Cockle's songs were well appreciated – indeed, it would be difficult to separate these vocalists as far as merit is concerned. Messrs Crabtree and Johnson were extremely successful with the humorous portion of the programme, their ditties evoking loud laughter.

'Too much praise cannot be given to Charlie Pledger for the way he must have worked in conjunction with Will Cotterell and their committees to bring about such a successful day.'

As the years went by, the 'flying balls' of lawn tennis would make Wimbledon famous around the world…

***

'I'd rather be fat than ugly.'

Mr Fat Wig stood back, confident that he had served a winning verbal volley. It was coming up to 11.30am on a summer Sunday morning. For the previous hour and a quarter, I had been part of one of Britain's great cultural traditions: the queue. Mention Wimbledon to the proverbial man on the bus, and his first thoughts may well be of the annual championships, which are the most famous tournament in world tennis. For a fortnight in late June and early July, the world's best players descend on the All England Lawn Tennis & Croquet Club in Church Road. Thousands of spectators watch, while depleting the European strawberry mountain. But, to get in, they have to queue.

So that was what I had been doing since just after 10a.m., queuing. I was determined to attain a Zen-like calm, as I knew it would take a while to get into the grounds. A few weeks before, an old acquaintance had given me advice. He had been a volunteer steward at the event for 20 years, only giving up a couple of years before my visit.

'Don't go early in the day,' he said.' Everything is at its busiest then. Try getting in sometime in late afternoon... four or five o'clock, perhaps.'

Would it be best to avoid a day when Britain's Andy Murray was playing in the singles?

'Go in the second week. He'll be out of the tournament by then!'

His advice was based on many years of national disappointment. No British man had won the Wimbledon singles, or even reached the final, since before World War II. Tim Henman had teased a nation by getting to the semi-finals, but no further, four times. Andy Murray promised to be the latest incarnation of that old adage about hope being worse than despair.

I had taken my friend's advice to some extent, by choosing the men's singles finals day for my visit. Murray had gone out, but not in the first week. Like Henman, he made it to the semi-finals, to continue the glorious British sporting tradition of near-misses. He was doomed to fall short, as soon as Gordon Brown sent a message wishing him luck on behalf of the whole nation.

Leaving the Underground at Southfields rather than Wimbledon, I had walked to the end of the queue, in the middle of a park that adjoins the tennis club, and received my numbered queue card, which would be proof of my position. A young, slim blonde steward in a fluorescent green tabard broke off from cheering the emergence of the sun from behind the clouds, to give me a booklet: *A Guide to Queueing for the Championships*. I declined the offer of a sticker, shaped like a strawberry, which said, 'I queued for Wimbledon.' It didn't seem much of a boast.

The booklet, though, was a great idea. I'd brought a chunky paperback with which to pass any dull moments, or half hours. The booklet was better. The title was a masterly piece of British understatement; the booklet included much information about the long term plans for developing the grounds, conditions of entry, where to eat and drink and shop, how to get tickets for the following year and so on. What raised the booklet above the level of more mundane, everyday, mortal booklets was the section on The Queue. In particular, my eye was drawn to 'The Queue Code of Conduct'.

Now, I've seen some strange things. Working in local government and further education guarantees that. I've never seen a code of conduct for a queue. Still, the organisers must know what they were doing.

'*Your position in the queue cannot be reserved by the placing of equipment – you must be present in person and hold a valid, numbered and dated Queue Card.*'

I hadn't thought of reserving my place using equipment. But now that the Code of Conduct mentioned it… in 20 or 30 years time, perhaps holograms would be available. Until then, a cardboard cut-out of me would have to do. It could be housed in a small box, which I would programme to rotate by a few degrees every ten minutes, to give a life-like impression.

'*Pizza/"take-away" orders must be arranged for delivery at the Wimbledon Park Road gate.*'

Did this mean I had to order a pizza? This was Wimbledon's equivalent of the London Underground signs which state: 'Dogs must be carried', leading me to wonder where and how I was going to acquire a dog. After much thought, I decided to ignore the All England Lawn Tennis & Croquet Club's stricture about pizzas and takeaways. I wasn't hungry. In all likelihood, a CCTV camera would film me failing to order a pizza or takeaway, and the evidence would be used to bar me from any future visits to the Club. I was willing to take the risk.

I looked up at the person ahead of me in the queue, a Japanese girl in her twenties, in a purple summer dress, carrying a white canvas bag with the words RED, GREEN, BLUE, ORANGE shown in their respective colours. She wasn't ordering a pizza, or placing illicit equipment to reserve her place, or doing anything else forbidden under the Code of Conduct. Nor, as far as the eye could see ahead of me or behind me, was anyone else. Nor did anyone else appear to be reading the booklet and its Code of Conduct.

So we all proceeded, moving at a slow but steady pace out of the field, along the road and towards the Club. Cheerful lollipop-shaped information boards informed us, at regular intervals, how many hundreds of yards we were from the main entrance. A freestanding mini-tent profiled some of the greatest champions from years gone past, and invited us to admire their portraits as painted by Rolf Harris. Thoughtful sponsor companies handed out free bottles of mineral water and cartons of watermelon juice, to keep us going.

I was close to being close to the entrance, when Mr Fat Wig accosted me. I had managed to avoid the attentions, a few hundred yards before, of two younger fundraisers who had been selling raffle tickets for a prize draw in aid of Save the Children. This time I wasn't so lucky. The man was not much more than five feet tall, and so comfortably built that no football fan would have had to ask who had eaten all the pies. He was wearing a white T-shirt that failed to cover his midriff whenever he moved, and shorts that were under considerable strain.

With one hand he rattled a bucket into which we were supposed to deposit our cash; with the other, he brandished an object that was a cross between a household duster and the type of tickling stick that Ken Dodd used to deploy. Its multi-coloured hue was a perfect match for the frizzy wig that covered his balding head.

Perhaps he wouldn't have spotted me if I hadn't turned to look at him, after his umpteenth rendition of: 'Children with Alzheimer's! Children with Alzheimer's!' but he did spot me. He waited until I was level with where he stood, poked at my shoulder with his duster-cum-tickling stick and pronounced:

'Cheer up, Cedric!'

At the risk of being over-analytical:

1. I am not called Cedric. I have never met anyone called Cedric, unless you count a beetle that used to scuttle across the living room floor of the first house we lived in after getting married. My wife and me, that is. Obviously I wouldn't marry a beetle. Anyway, we called it Cedric. I have no idea why.

2. I didn't think I was looking that unhappy at the time.

3. If anything is guaranteed to make anyone unhappy, it is someone who doesn't know you telling you to cheer up.

4. Being poked with a duster-cum-tickling stick, while being told to cheer up, does not enhance the effectiveness of the advice.

All this passed through my head, a nanosecond before I replied, 'Pick on someone your own size.'

It's not Oscar Wilde standard, I know, and it's not fair to draw attention to a person's stature if they are anorexically challenged. But it was the best I could do at the time.

Mr Fat Wig was not used to his pokes and advice being challenged. He gave me an indignant stare and retorted, 'I *am* your size.'

This might have been true in a hall of mirrors, but nowhere else. By dint of the international language of mime, I drew his attention to his Orinoco-like girth.

Although the queue continued to move, at about the same pace of Cedric across our living room floor, I was not quite beyond Mr Fat Wig's range. He pulled himself up to his full height. This did not take long, enabling him to fire his parting shot, 'I'd rather be fat than ugly.'

I gave this a moment's thought. Mr Fat Wig was older, fatter, balder and shorter than me so, in the circumstances, he needed some advice.

'I'd consult an optician if I were you,' I told him.

His mouth flopped open and stayed there. If only I'd had a tennis ball to hand. But the queue was moving again, so I left him there. Next time your children ask you, 'Why are people rude to other people?' you can say, 'Well, darling, sometimes they deserve it. And it can be fun.'

After two hours in a slow-moving queue, I arrived at the All England Club… or, at least, at the security check point. One of the perverse benefits of waiting so long is that you're pleased to see anyone within those hallowed grounds even if they are checking whether you're a terrorist, or a suicide spectator, or whatever.

'Do you mind if I look in your wallet?' asked the amiable, tall young man in lane F. I invited him to do so, and to let me know if he found anything of value.

In order to speed up the security checks, there were eight separate lanes dealing with visitors, just like my local supermarket. I looked in vain for the 'Six offensive weapons or less' lane before going to lane F. There were other similarities, too. It's a staple of a visit to Tesco to reach the checkout and encounter a staff member whose bedtime came and went hours ago. They run your goods through the barcode machine, which emits an error message, and then shout at a fellow member of staff, who should be queuing for their pension, to go to the relevant shelf and check the price of the items. The young man searching my wallet at the All England Club might have been 12 or, at a pinch, 17; the stewards patrolling inside the Club could have escaped from *Last of the Summer Wine*. If it were up to me, I'd put the old blokes on the checkout (or checkpoint) and get the young ones to do the walking or running around, but that's much too sensible.

Once I got in, the experience of walking round Wimbledon was surreal. The Club is shaped like a closed quotation mark and contains 19 tennis courts, a bank, a newsagent, a museum, shops and a tea lawn with bandstand and champagne bar not to mention ten other bars, cafés and restaurants. This was not a surprise, as an information board along the queuing route had told me that a typical Wimbledon fortnight saw the consumption of 8,000 litres of Robinson's barley water, 135,000 ice creams and 300,000 cups of tea. As I had arrived two hours before the start of the men's singles final (or "Gentlemen's", as the Club calls it), there was far more eating and drinking to see than tennis. Resisting the call of half a lobster – which would have cost half my mortgage – I sustained myself with a Cornish pasty.

One of my proudest boasts – all right, one of my few boasts of any validity – is that I was at the Oval in 2005 when the England men's cricket team regained the Ashes against Australia. Unless the national football team wins a major tournament, I don't expect to encounter that level of tension and excitement again at a sporting event. It wasn't there at Wimbledon, that's for sure.

There was no direct British interest but, even so, the laidback mood surprised me. The decor might have something to do with it. The purple/green colour combination had a whiff of girls' school uniforms to it. The other reason was, irony of ironies, that I had arrived too late in the tournament. Early in the fortnight, all the courts are in use; there is plenty to see. By the final Sunday, as its name implies, there are only some finals left. Sole security men sit, looking disconsolate, in the stands of courts 7 and 9 and 13 and 17. The final day of every other major sporting event I can think of would see a packed stadium but, at Wimbledon, ninety per cent of the place is empty.

Court 4, though, was busy with the finals of the women's 'DW', as the information screen told me. DW turned out to be 'double wheelchairs', with four women players firing forehands, backhands, serves and volleys like lasers.

'WHY WOULD YOU DO THAT?' screamed one of the women at herself, as she hit a shot into the net. I thought she was being hard on herself.

It was all a far cry from my brief, unsuccessful tennis career at school, when I tried to serve the ball through the extra-large holes in the net and hoped nobody would notice. I applauded, and moved on towards the exit, past the strawberry mountains and the Pimm's lakes.

This one-fortnight-a-year purple and green interloper of an event was not, I decided, the true Wimbledon. That belonged to the families who had come to see Great Uncle Bulgaria, and who walked the Common with Ziggy and other dogs. But now it was time to move away from Wimbledon, to discover the places that gave the Wombles their names – beginning with a South American river...

ORINOCO

As the canoe powered along, eating the miles and killing conversation, I wondered how I agreed to do this. River trips aren't for me. I need water-wings in the bath.

I've taken boat trips round Lake Maggiore, and up and down the Thames, but in large groups. My cousin had all the water sports genes of the family – he rowed for London University. (I wanted, as a small boy, to see Simon in the Boat Race and couldn't understand why it always featured Oxford and Cambridge.) But this was a small blue motorised canoe with four occupants: Ales (pronounced Alex), our guide, Chendo the navigator, Helen and me.

Four people sitting in one boat, on the widest river I have ever seen. The surface seemed calm, but the water wasn't empty.

In the face of fear, it's traditional to think of the loved ones you have left behind. In this case, Helen was in the boat next to me – saying nothing as her shoulder-length fair hair got two years worth of blow-dries in one instalment. So, instead of loved ones, maybe I'd think of exactly what to say to my boss when I got back to work. If I got back.

***

A few days earlier, we were standing outside what looked like a garage lockup. The driver seemed to have confused number 8 on one street with number 30 on another. Helen had shown him our travel plans, but that made no difference. He was convinced he knew where our hotel was, but nobody was answering the door and there was nobody on the street to ask.

This puzzle was our introduction to Ciudad Bolívar, capital of Venezuela's south-eastern Bolívar state, which is set on the banks of the Orinoco. The city used to be called Angostura, back in the early 19th century when it had a ringside seat at the Venezuelans' struggle for independence. It was in Angostura that Dr Siegert, a surgeon-general in Simón Bolívar's army, developed and started to sell, in 1824, a tonic solution that took its name from the city and achieved worldwide fame.

Angostura changed its name in honour of Bolívar, the general whose forces liberated Venezuela, Peru, Ecuador, Bolivia and New Granada (later known as Colombia) from Spain. The Congress of Angostura of 1819 heralded a new era for Venezuela. But, as we would find out, after that dream start, things could only get bitter.

We weren't too happy ourselves as we waited for a solution to the mystery of the missing hotel. I looked up and down the street. Parked across the road from number 8, by a kerb of ankle-breaking height, was a red Toyota with white designer paw prints on its bonnet. There seemed to be an explosion of colour spots on the pavement. I looked closer. They were paint spots.

I looked up. The house where the Toyota was parked had a magenta façade with turquoise doors, and iron bars in a diamond pattern across the window shutters. This was not the only extrovert house on the street. Its neighbour was cream with green doors. Like a Pantone addict, I was hooked.

Further up the street, an ochre house with royal blue doors; then very pale pink with British racing green doors and bars; burnt orange with lilac doors and black bars; apricot with British racing green doors. I've liked British racing green ever since I saw it on my uncle's 1929 vintage

Riley, which he used to race for fun. Family legend had it that he kept the components in jam jars in between races.

All the houses were square, with flat roofs giving them a squat appearance. Without the arrays of colours on their facades, they might have resembled prison blocks. Halfway back up the hill was an old-fashioned lamp with an energy-efficient light bulb.

A solution was at hand for our mystery, in the shape of a burly man with a greying beard and a T-shirt bearing the legend 'EQ'. He explained that number 8 was a hotel, but not the one that we wanted, which was round the corner. A short woman in her forties, with a rumpled dark blouse and skirt, appeared and led us to what seemed to be another lock-up.

Like the other building, there was no sign that it was a hotel. Our hostess turned the key to open the outside gate and ushered us through an anteroom into the courtyard of a colonial-era *pasada* (inn). The typewriter on the reception desk, the railway station-style clock above the door and the telephone in the corner would all have been familiar to my grandparents. On the other hand, the mini-chapel in the far corner, and the grappling hook at the far end of the courtyard, might have puzzled them. A small fountain in the middle of a mini-pool guarded by a plastic ibis provided the gentle cascade of running water which is calm and soothing, or makes you want to visit the bathroom, depending on your taste.

It was time to hit the streets. We took a couple of turnings from the hotel into Plaza Bolívar. One country (Bolivia), a state in another country, a city and now a city square; all named after Simón Bolívar or, to give him his full name, Simón José Antonio de la Santísima Trinidad Bolívar Palacios y Blanco. It's just as well that Elisabeth Beresford named the Wombles after places rather than people. A five minute episode about Simón wouldn't have had time for anything apart from the credits.

Simón's family, from Spain, settled in Venezuela in the 16th century and he was born in Caracas in 1783. His mother and father died before he reached the age of nine, so he went to Spain for much of his childhood and education. There he married María in 1802 but, on a brief return visit to Venezuela in 1803, she succumbed to yellow fever. Bolívar returned to Europe the following year and for a time was part of Napoleon's retinue, before returning to Venezuela.

The next decade saw Simón rise to command armies that invaded Venezuela, New Granada (modern Colombia) and elsewhere. Their successes included the capture of Angostura in 1817 with the help of soldiers and aid from Haiti. By 1821 Gran Colombia (a federation covering much of modern Venezuela, Colombia, Panama, and Ecuador) had been created, with Bolívar as president. He became dictator of a liberated Peru in 1824 and Bolivia was created in 1825.

However, what took over ten years to create took less than half that time to fall apart. Regional interests and loyalties proved too strong. Bolívar proclaimed himself dictator in 1828, but that didn't work. Assassination attempts followed, as did further uprisings in New Granada, Venezuela and Ecuador.

Bolívar resigned the Presidency in despair in 1830, and made plans to exile himself to Europe. Tuberculosis got him before he got the boat, and he died in Santa Marta that December at the age of 47. The Venezuelan government made him a posthumous *persona non grata* until 1842, when it returned his remains to Caracas and erected a monument in his honour. He has been a national hero ever since.

As Helen and I sauntered into Plaza Bolívar that Sunday, we would, no doubt, have had a cheerful welcome, if anyone had been around. It was just the statues and us. Bolívar was in the centre, all stern expression and epaulettes. There might not have been much time for laughter in his life – another day, another country to liberate. Perhaps he looked stern because the locals hadn't erected this statue until 1869.

Five neo-classical female statues surrounded him, each representing one of the nations he liberated. They had blank expressions on their faces and carried shields with all manner of things such as horses, mountains, the moon, the sun and so on.

Such people as we could find were meandering around the historic buildings in the square. We started with Casa del Congreso de Angostura, a shocking pink building on the western side. The Congress met between 1819-1821, as revolution raged. Two soldiers who looked younger than their uniforms, and uncomfortable in their busbies, did their statue impressions either side of the entrance. A small girl in her teens asked us to sign the visitors' book – a common practice in Venezuela, as are requests for your ID (i.e. passport) number as well as your name. The rooms were full of worthy 19th century portraits, except for one colourful modern mural above a piano. The men in the mural all had Bolívar-style sideburns, serious expressions and seemed to be versatile in the art of hand signals.

Casa Piar on the northern side of the square has a blue painted brick exterior, with little or nothing to identify it until you go into the entry hall. It commemorates a general who won key battles for Venezuela's independence, but refused to submit to Bolívar's rule. He was executed by firing squad, with Bolívar watching from across the square. A plaque on the wall of the square quotes Bolívar praising General Piar, five months before Piar's execution… I enjoyed the mural which attempted a Venezuelan interpretation of the four horsemen of the apocalypse (there were three, with crude shapes for heads without any of those nice optional extras like eyes, ears or a nose). As we left Casa Piar, the first thing we saw was the statue of Bolívar, staring Piar down even in death.

Back at the hotel, things were quiet and dark, giving the courtyard an unsettling quality. Only two other people were staying there apart from us. It turned out that number 8 – although not our hotel – was a partner of number 30, and it was our destination for dinner. Having to ring the bell for the hotel door to be opened was a little unnerving. One meal of asparagus soup, catfish and watermelon later, I wanted to try the Plaza again; things might be hotting up. That was what happened in Spain, after all. The hotel manageress looked askance as we turned right out of number 8.

'Where are you going?'

'To Plaza Bolívar.'

'Oh…well, be careful…it isn't very safe around here.'

Helen and I looked at each other, shrugged and promised the manageress we would look out for what Helen's father used to call 'road agents' (I don't know what he meant, 20 years after first hearing the term). Nothing occurred, good, bad or indifferent, with the square still empty. Half an hour later, we returned to our room and there was a knock on the door. It was the manageress, checking that we were all right. That spooked me more than her original warning.

The next morning, on our way down to the riverside, we went back to Plaza Bolívar for one last attempt to find some life. This time, we were in luck. A service appeared to be going on in the cathedral, although the music was not of the traditional Western genre, and bursts of applause erupted from time to time. In a corner, next to the Peru statue, a group of young boys were putting on stilts. The boys' outfits, topped off with knotted handkerchiefs around their heads, combined shades of orange, green, yellow and blue, as if they were performing for the annual conference of highlighter pen salesmen. The boys started to walk around Peru, for practice. Teams of cleaners in red T-shirts, baseball caps and shorts ambled around the square, making judicious use of dustpans and brushes.

The cathedral service ended and people filed out, chatting animatedly. Two men in black suits hefted a floral bouquet. They set it up in front of the statue of Bolívar. Meanwhile, from the far corner of the square, a crocodile of schoolboys in blue shirts and black trousers appeared and started to file towards the cathedral entrance.

The cathedral congregation seemed to be following the lead of a tall man in a blue suit. His spectacles, short, greying hair and beard gave him a resemblance to Kofi Annan, former secretary-general of the UN. He gathered people together in front of the Bolívar statue and the wreath for photos, while a short man in a blue jacket and check trousers appeared to be recording a commentary of some type, for the benefit of a cameraman. I had been wary of taking photos – partly because it wasn't a good way to stay inconspicuous and partly because, if this was some type of major local event, Kofi might not want *gringos* capturing it on film. However, nobody cared about Helen and me, they were busy posing.

The stilt-walkers chose this moment to advance on the cathedral goers. *Oh no*, I thought… *this isn't the time for a public performance. The men in black mean this must have been a funeral or memorial service or something… a circus act is the last thing they want right now.*

Then the stilt-walkers began to move out of the square and up the hill, clapping their hands rhythmically and chanting. Kofi, the men in black and the rest of the congregation followed them in a slow and cheerful procession. It was all connected after all… apart from the schoolboys, who filed into the cathedral for what sounded, a few minutes later, like choir practice. The cleaners had gone, too. Apart from the floral wreath by the Bolívar statue, everything was as it had been before: just the statues and us.

We turned left out of the square, going along Calle Constitucion, downhill towards the river, taking care not to fall from the vertiginous kerb into the road. The local cars were either land cruiser monsters or small models for one-person shopping trips; all were either new or ancient. Some of the windscreen wipers might have been made from Meccano. The number plates specified the country and the state of origin, which was in most cases (surprise, surprise) Bolívar.

The houses on Calle Constitucion bore paler variations of the bright colours from the street where we were staying. Hanging from some of them were little stars, wreaths of holly and – in one case – some mini-Santas. It might be late January, but it was still Christmas in Ciudad Bolívar, it seemed.

And at Christmas you eat…hot cross buns? That was the smell wafting from somewhere near the riverfront as we made it down to Paseo Orinoco, the main street by the river. Some of the shops were hedging their bets. One boasted piles of mattresses on the first floor and an array of gleaming new motorbikes for sale on the ground floor. I wondered if the owners would consider my idea for a name for their shop. Easy Rider seemed like a winner to me. I had the neighbouring shop down as a sports store until I noticed the clocks and lamps cluttering up one side of the display.

Other outlets did specialise. My non-existent Spanish had me thinking that the *ferreteria* could supply me with the late Richard Whiteley's nemesis, but it was an ironmonger's. An electrical and electronics shop offered Wii, car radios, hair clippers, phones, irons, food processors and more. On the pavement, a man at a red table was mending mobile phones or fitting new batteries, doing his best to ignore the cacophony of *merengue* music blaring from the sunglasses stall. In a parking space near a zebra crossing, the lower half of an unclad female mannequin stood, alone.

We crossed the road to Mirador Orinoco, a large hut-style bar, to pause for a cool drink. Parents wheeled prams past, pensioners sat by the riverside looking into space and we tried to guess which 80s song the bar would play next. *Nights in White Satin* did not suit the blue skies and bright sun, and a *Careless Whisper* would not have been heard above the chatter of conversations and the market stall cries of vendors promoting the merits of today's bananas. You could only describe it as hectic if you compared it with Sunday afternoon, but I was reassured that we hadn't landed in a ghost town.

Out of the historic centre in downtown Ciudad Bolívar, the Botanical Gardens seemed to be a secret. By standing around looking gormless, we managed to get a free guided tour of the private section, from Felix – a young man from Brazil who went to a US university to get a Master's degree in education and art, then married a Venezuelan. Among the contents of the private section were a baobab, a cockroach plant (so called because its spiky purple flowers remind people of the local roaches), bromeliads (very valuable status symbols in Venezuela, which can fetch up to $300 a time) and a lake in the middle, inhabited by a cayman which had lunched on a snake donated to the gardens. Propagation of the plants was by seeds and cuttings, many of them in plastic drinks cups – an irony, or a Womble-like way to use old rubbish?

We said goodbye to Ciudad Bolívar by eating an *arepa* – a corn pancake, split and stuffed with chicken – in a café where diners sat in a reserved area behind a secure gate. The stereotype of the sleepy Latin-Caribbean town didn't seem to match up to a place where diners ate, and dogs barked, behind bars.

***

On the other hand, you can have too much freedom. Some nice, strong bars on either side of the motorised canoe, or windows, might have been good – something to stop me falling into the Orinoco. There weren't even any seatbelts.

The river was calm, given the speed at which we ploughed through it. Our luggage was stowed away at the front. How much we put our trust in total strangers, I thought. Ales or Chendo could be useless seamen. They could be murderers or conmen.

A boat passed in the opposite direction; I resisted a temptation to shout 'CAMBRIDGE!'

Memories surfaced of the first time I managed to swim a width of the school pool. It was supposed to be a length but the teacher took pity, and so did my classmates, judging by their ironic applause as I touched the far side. Here on the Orinoco, it had to be 20 pool widths to the riverbank on either side, or 30, or 100. For the millionth time I told myself not to exaggerate.

This was not the type of transfer I am used to. I can sleep well in cars, much to Helen's annoyance as I miss the scenery. Once we were being chauffeured through a rocky, barely-there mountain road in Albania and I slept through every swerve and brake and dip.

'Were you expecting a road as bad as this?' asked the interpreter.

'I was expecting a road,' Helen replied in Lady Bracknell mode.

On planes there are nibbles, and if you're lucky there's a map showing how many thousands of miles to go to your destination. There's a magazine and an in-flight film or two. On the way to Caracas we saw *Scoop* – Woody Allen's fantasy comedy that culminates in a drowning scene in a lake. Oh dear... shouldn't have mentioned that.

So – no windscreen, no seatbelts, no sick bag, no safety demonstration, no film, no nibbles. There was a lifejacket, but I'd put it on the wrong way round.

Ales looked out front with a blank expression. Then he pointed to the riverbank on our left, and Chendo killed the engine. Was this some rendezvous with contract killers, perhaps? I wondered how much money an English couple would fetch. The exchange rate trends meant we were worth less than a week ago.

I saw what Ales had seen: two large shapes in the treetops. Red howler monkeys were sitting there, with unfathomable facial expressions. The boat sat there for a while on the quiet river, until another gesture from Ales got Chendo to gun the engine and move us off.

We reached the lodge and I leapt for the jetty with the grace of... no, there is no applicable simile or metaphor, there was no grace. But I hadn't drowned, which was a good start.

***

This was our home for the next three nights. Under the big thatched roof was the main area of the lodge. The bar on the left bore the name Yakaro (this means 'good' in Warao, the local dialect). A sign bid us 'BIENVENIDOS'. A T-shirt with a photo of Barack Obama hung in the back. The bar stools had blue seats and green legs. Speakers were tied to the wall by ropes. Close to the bar was a small table with a sign 'INTERNET AVAILABLE', next to a laptop that had, as Eric Morecambe might have said, all the right components but not necessarily in the right order.

Further back, to the right of the bar, was a mural of a blue and gold macaw, below a whiteboard with advice for enjoying our stay (e.g. 'close your cabin door quickly if you don't want to share it with mosquitoes'). A head-high sign had the words 'FOX NEWS', crossed out.

We edged past a bicycle and water cooler, and glanced inside the office. 'Office' was underselling it, to be fair. The room contained two desks, two bookcases, boxes of other stuff, two phones, two faxes, a deep freeze and a fire extinguisher lodged, at a jaunty angle, into the wire frame which formed the office wall. Get any people in there, and it would have been crowded. Next to the office, piles of wellies sat awaiting their next wearers.

In the centre of the main area of the lodge was an open section with several coffee tables, chairs and wooden sofas with blue and caramel cushions. A large sign proclaimed 'ORINOCO DELTA LODGE'. Several paintings hung from the wall, each ten feet high: a portrait of a young Warao girl; a modern skyscraper city in a triangular spaceship blasting off into space; an explorer in a safari suit, seated at a desk talking into an old-fashioned phone with toucans, tigers, crocodiles and other animals surrounding him. A small information stand told us about the local school, and appealed for money to fund a second teacher.

On the right of the area was a toilet, with its own thatched roof. Another sign told us that 'Life goes on'. Beyond dining tables of various shapes was the kitchen, with its own green and caramel façade. An eagle was sitting in the awnings above the kitchen, waiting for the chicken meal which Lodge staff had provided to defrost.

Throughout the main area were pillars painted a random selection of navy blue, turquoise, banana-yellow and strawberry-pink. Red crazy paving floor tiles led out of the left and right of the main area, to raised walkways with cabins on stilts on either side. We were staying in number 18, next door to the puma.

We didn't see much of our neighbour, as she padded in and out of the pools of water in her cage. But she made an impact on our nights. All that padding must have been tiring work. She snored like a foghorn, for hours. We would have banged on the wall in complaint, but as it was made of mosquito netting that wouldn't have done much good.

The puma's snores were part of the night-time soundtrack. As the lodge's power cut out at the appointed time of 11p.m., extinguishing the sole light bulb in the centre of our cabin, a chorus of frogs and insects serenaded us.

After the frogs came the dogs, who revealed themselves in daytime as mongrels of various types and colours.

The honey-coloured largest member of the pack had a nickname 'the Doctor' for his habit of sniffing everyone and everything to check nothing was amiss. The black-and-white bitzer with floppy ears ran in front of his fellow canines, the cats and the humans, fixing them all with penetrating stares. He could have been a police dog: he thought he was in charge, sniffing the little white poodle lookalike all round the lodge. As to which one kept up the night-time barking for two hours, my two *bolívars* were on the poodle (even the currency paid homage to old Simón).

Just as the mystery barker gave up, somewhere between two and three in the morning, and I tossed and turned into what I hoped would be a sleeping position, the cockerels started. I could do nothing except grumble and visualise the judicious use of a shotgun and a delicious chicken dinner.

Another guest had arrived at the lodge the day before – Marc, an amiable Swiss version of Johnny Vegas, taking four weeks away from his job in informatics. The three of us had gone for a late afternoon boat trip. Purple *bora* reeds floated up and down the river for six hours at a time in each direction, according to the tide. Parrots took the same route each evening, flying in pairs from the more open side of the river, where they spent the day, to the more jungle-intensive side where they roosted. After I had snatched some sleep, my first sight on waking was the *bora* reeds floating past our cabin. I had a momentary disorientation: the *bora* couldn't be travelling that fast – our cabin had moved. It turned out that it could, and we hadn't.

Marc, Helen and I had the chance of a jungle walk, although a jungle squelch would be a better description. The heavy rain that morning made our tasteful yellow wellies essential for staying upright. Chendo went ahead, clearing a path with a machete. He hacked off a plant stem, tipped it up and tasted the liquid within – it was, in something of an anticlimax, just like water. Another plant's fruit was round and hard, with brown knobbles on the outside; the fruit of the *moriche*, or oily palm. The taste reminded us of kiwi fruit. Ales demonstrated how to climb liana and we declined his invitation to try.

Back in the boat, we moved down the river, with the occasional parrot flying overhead and electric blue butterflies as large as my hand dancing either side of us. After miles of 20 metre tall trees on either side, we reached an area of low-growing reeds and open sky. This was our location for a spot of piranha fishing.

I was expecting a pep talk or some top tips or tall fishing tales, to encourage us. Ales and Chendo gave us what we needed, and started casting. The Orinoco technique for fishing is easy to describe. You take a long stick with a piece of twine, a hook and a piece of white meat as bait. Then you stick the bait in the water and thrash the rod around, churning up the water and making the maximum possible noise to attract the attention of fish.

This was a fishing party without a track record. Neither Helen nor I had fished before. (As a small boy, I had won a goldfish on Hampstead Heath, by tossing three balls into a bucket. He was called Pete and he didn't enjoy the drive home, and he lived another eight months.) Marc refused to eat fish, but agreed to come on the trip.

Fifteen minutes went by as if they were an hour. The only noise on the river was our makeshift rods, as we thrashed them around in the manner of guitar heroes. It was Helen who noticed that something had been nibbling at her bait. We redoubled our thrashing efforts.

Ales caught a piranha, then Helen followed suit with a red variation. I took a photo, capturing the details of the fierce eyes, the sharp teeth and the deadly expression of a killer. I made sure the piranha got in the photo, too. Ales unhooked it and threw it into the back row of the canoe seating, where it performed an involuntary breakdance as its death throes.

Ales caught his second. Chendo landed a red piranha large enough to be the mother of Helen's prize. Marc had been no luckier than me, until he lodged his hook in a piranha's gills.

All this time I had had no sniff of a catch, apart from a nearby bush that I snagged, pulling myself close to the water in the type of accident that befell Orinoco in every Wombles story. Maybe I didn't have the touch, the eyesight, the talent or whatever it was that anglers needed.

Then there was a huge pull on my line. I didn't react at first: an hour of nothing had dulled my reactions. But I pulled myself together and pulled the rod. Whatever it was resisted, hard.

This was it, the largest piranha in the West, and a hearty supper with enough photos and stories to bore for twenty years. Or perhaps it was a catfish. Or…

I pulled harder and faster…and the rod snapped in two, halfway up. I received no sympathy. The others fell around laughing.

'You caught a large twig,' said Ales. 'Or maybe it was the bottom of the boat.'

In my heart of hearts I knew it had been a big fish. In my heart of heart of hearts, I knew it had been a boot or a stray branch. My brief angling career came to an end as we rode back to the lodge in driving rain, sheltering under a big plastic sheet.

***

I've no idea how many plane journeys I've taken in my life. And I have no idea why I'm so surprised and outraged when the plane is late in taking off. In Venezuela, the congruence of Latin America and the Caribbean makes *mañana* a starting point for negotiations, and the day after *mañana* is a better bet for getting anything done.

So it came to pass that our internal flight from Puerto Ordaz to Caracas took off nearly two hours late,.and landed late after a bout of circling, due to rain. To get over the excitement, the authorities allowed us to sit in a bus on the runway for 15 minutes before entering the terminal.

Plenty of carousels awaited our luggage, but no signs told us which one we should head for. In a disorientated state, we found the luggage and headed for Felix, our guide who had greeted us in Caracas a week before, and who was here for our final day in the country.

He was a reassuring sight, a bearded man in his forties with greying hair and a slim figure hidden beneath a baseball cap, a high-visibility tabard and jeans. He flashed a cavernous smile. Many Venezuelans, including Felix, eschew the horizontal-to-horizontal handshake. They bring their hand down from the vertical, swooping until you're not sure whether they want to shake your hand or rap your knuckles, gangster-style.

We updated Felix on our adventures as we walked towards the exit for the car park. Yes, we had enjoyed the holiday. No, we hadn't taken his advice to use vitamin B to ward off insect bites. Yes, we now had peeling red skin in various places as well as the bites. Yes, I would be happy to show Felix the photographs of our stay.

I felt for my shoulder bag. It wasn't on my shoulder. I wasn't carrying it. Helen wasn't carrying it. Felix wasn't carrying it. It wasn't on Helen's shoulder. It wasn't on Felix's shoulder. Nobody else in sight had swiped it. I knew where the bag wasn't. I knew where I was… in trouble.

The blood drained from my face, I looked at Helen's expression and wondered whether I would get to find out if any of the airport shops supplied divorce kits (while you wait). Several hundred pounds worth of camera, with a week's worth of photos, were in that bag.

Felix stayed calm. We took the lift back down to the carousels and he persuaded security to let me look for the bag. It was still there, on the floor where I'd left it.

'You are lucky,' said Felix.

I restrained myself from doing a Gene Kelly in the steady rain outside. After several triple checks that we had loaded each and every bag into Felix's car, he drove into the city towards our hotel. As traffic thickened, the car started hiccupping.

'It must be water in the engine,' said Felix, calm as calm could be. 'The car has never done this before.'

The hiccups passed. We tried to think peaceful thoughts as heavy traffic around the baseball stadium before a game held us up. A man stepped into the road. Felix wound down his window. The man tried to sell Felix a pink baseball cap branded Caracas Leones. Felix said he already had one, so the man suggested that Felix buy one for his wife. Some smiling and joking later, the vendor did not make a sale and we moved on.

The car resumed its hiccupping as we entered Avenue Casanova, near the hotel.

'I am so sorry,' said Felix, worry entering his voice. 'I want to ask a favour. My wife's office is nearby, with a car park. We can park the car there. It is only a few hundred yards from your hotel.'

As we turned the corner to find the office and car park, a dark-haired woman in a bra, knickers, tights and very little else glared at us from the pavement. Felix found the car park, and he and a security guard helped us with our bags as we walked to the hotel, past crowds of people and cars blaring out deafening pop music. We had been warned that while the hotel was high quality, it was in a dangerous part of the city. There was no sign of any more underdressed ladies, although I might have missed them as I was keeping a close eye on the luggage.

Our plan was to book in, have a hot shower, raid the minibar, order room service and go to bed. Felix gave us a final swooping handshake and went off to get a train home to see his two daughters. His wife was on a business trip to Brazil and Felix had been growing anxious as the car's travails threatened to disrupt his parental schedule.

The reception staff stopped admiring themselves in their Nehru suits for long enough to confirm our booking, give us a room key and direct us to the third floor. Once in the lift, I spent a few minutes failing to discover that I had to put the room key into the lift controls, otherwise we would not be moving in either direction all night. We reached our room in the best hotel in Caracas, a 'Leading Hotel of the World'. Everything would run like clockwork from now on, I was sure.

I looked at the large bed and wondered why three pillows were lined up side by side. I thought of the woman on the pavement, and shuddered. The air-conditioning followed the standard rule of air-conditioning: it's either noisy or it doesn't work. This one was noisy. We couldn't find an off switch, so Helen pulled the plug out before making for the shower.

There was no mini-bar. A huge cabinet concealed a TV with dozens of channels, all in Spanish except CNN International. I switched off *Larry King Live* and perused the room service menu.

A shriek of agony rent the air. Helen had found out that the shower wasn't so much a power shower as a nuclear power shower. One touch released a torrent of water that could scald.

I rang for room service. A female voice explained:

'I am sorry, sir. In order to have room service, you must deposit some money at the reception, then phone us again.'

Call me pedantic... that isn't room service. That's room-then-down-to-reception-then-back-to-room service. Still, I went to get my wallet. I looked down and noticed that the carpet, in our bedroom in a Leading Hotel of the World, was nailed down. At reception, Marlyn – a charming girl, aged about 12 - asked for a deposit of 300 *bolívars*, three times as much as I was expecting to spend on the meal. I negotiated this down to 100 *bolívars* and returned to room 325 to order our meal. In my absence, a furious row had broken out in the next room. Mutual shrieking and shouting in French entertained us until room service arrived.

There was plenty to eat for breakfast the next morning. I've always wanted to pretend to be Egon Ronay or a hotel inspector. As waiting staff smiled nervous smiles, I noted the following options in my black notebook:

Assorted sliced cheese
Sweet French pastries
Pastry with ham and cheese inside
Croissants
Bread rolls, with Kerrygold butter on the side
Sauvignon blanc
Yoghurts
Chocolate marble cake
Mini-profiteroles and mini-cakes
Waffles
Pancakes
Chocolate syrup
Strawberry syrup
Maple syrup
Toaster and bread slices
Oat Meal [sic]
Skimmed milk
Whole milk
Cornflakes
Special K
All Bran
Muesli
Chocolate muesli
Diet jelly

Turkey ham
Crackers
Fruit salad
Chicken in Mediterranean sauce
Sausages
Fricadelly
Fried cornbread
Fried plantain
Grilled ham
Brussels sprouts
Black beans
Shredded meat
Scrambled eggs
Tortilla
Empanadas
Ham and cheese slices
Eggs fried (on request)
Misu [sic] soup
Guavas
Apples
Melons
Grapes
Bananas
Papaya
Grapefruit
Strawberries
Pears
Watermelon
Pineapple
Walnuts
Dried apricots
Raisins
Dry figs
Dry plums
Dry fruits with cereals
Guava with syrup

Peach in syrup
Figs in syrup
Oatmeal and fruit muesli
Condensed milk
Assorted cold meats

I gave up in the end – going round the breakfast made a jungle walk seem like a cakewalk – so I might have missed one or two things off the list. Still, it made a change to follow the food, rather than having it follow me.

***

Twenty-four hours beforehand, I'd been ducking and weaving to avoid an aerial assault. It was just outside our cabin at the lodge. I was contemplating the end of our stay on the Orinoco, and looking at nothing in particular. Marc had left the previous day, and other guests were not due until that evening. Helen and I were alone apart from the staff, and Helen was in the cabin, and not in the habit of shinning up trees in any case. So who was pelting me with the fruit of the *moriche* trees?

As more fruit splatted on the path, I looked up and caught a flash of gold. Of course… it was Rumba. We had been expecting to see crocodiles, hoping to catch piranhas and hoping we wouldn't see anaconda, spiders or scorpions. And there was our neighbour, the puma. The most dangerous inhabitant of the lodge, though, was a blue and gold macaw.

She didn't mean any harm. Rumba was enjoying her breakfast and dropping quantities of it from the tree. Isaac Newton's career might have had a premature end if he had been born in Venezuela.

Rumba did have some form, in terms of food dropping. The previous lunchtime, we had been enjoying catfish in coconut sauce. The table and our chairs were just tall enough to help us fend off the attention of two kittens, one ginger and the other black and white. The ginger kitten was attempting yet another heroic ascent of the north face of my leg, when a squawk exploded in my ear.

Rumba didn't waste time – her beak captured a piece of these pesky humans' lunch and set to work. She hopped onto the back of Helen's chair and parts of the ill-gotten gain fell down Helen's jacket. A few bits got into her bag, although we didn't suspect that at the time: not even an hour later, when Helen came across the police dog with its head in her bag. We thought it was checking for drugs.

Later that afternoon, Rumba sat on the door of the bar with a guilty expression, as if she'd been at the drinks. I made a few encouraging squawk noises. Rumba erupted off the door onto my right shoulder, and grasped my right cheek in her beak.

Saying nothing stronger than 'Ouch…ouch…ouch… ouch' a few dozen times, I persuaded myself that Rumba was being friendly. Perhaps she had been at the drinks, and this was the parrot equivalent of the drunken 'I rrrreally love you…you're my…best friend'.

By this time, Rumba had begun to take an interest in my arm, and was testing her beak on that. I kept my nerve and prayed she wouldn't draw blood. At length, she disengaged herself from me, in favour of a game of 'hide the sugar bowl' with Ales. Rumba had left nothing more than a couple of small marks, as a counterpoint to the many bites from the local midges.

Rumba resembled a five-year-old human, with her demands for attention and her disruptive tendencies. Talking of five-year-olds, we met some of them, at the primary school on the other side of the river. There was one main room, with a partition across the middle. On one side, the younger children of the Warao tribe sat on the floor, stared at a whiteboard and learned the Spanish

Rumba the parrot and (feline) friend

alphabet. On the other, the older children practised writing Spanish phrases such as 'my brother does the dishes' at desks-cum-chairs. One young female bilingual teacher took care of both groups.

Two girls sat cross-legged in what seemed to be party dresses, while others wore leggings the colour of a green highlighter, or jeans. Some went barefoot and others wore trainers. Like teachers anywhere, this one had her work cut out just to keep her charges' attention, as they indulged in foot fights (rather like the kittens in the lodge), giggling and jumping against the netting which served as walls. There was no sign of childhood obesity in any of them: no budding Orinocos here.

Break time saw a raid on a cupboard and the production of large white dice, which the children used to play a form of marbles or boules. There was plenty of noise, and no clock. On the blue and yellow walls were educational posters about trees, the human body and Simón Bolívar.

The following morning reminded us that Bolívar might have been the original popular dictator of Venezuela, but he had a modern counterpart: Hugo Chávez, the President since 1998. As Felix used his brother's car to take us round Caracas, the comparisons between the two became ever more explicit.

'Chávez is trying to rewrite the constitution,' said Felix as he drove us past dozens of people wielding 'Si' signs. 'He is holding a referendum on whether a president should be allowed to run for office more than twice. Chávez wants to be President for life.'

Over 175 years ago, Bolívar had proposed similar constitutional amendments, without success. Chávez had already proposed these changes in a referendum and had been defeated. But, unlike his hero Bolívar, Chávez was determined to try again with another referendum.

Chávez's story was as remarkable as Bolívar's. After 17 years in military service, he had gone to jail in 1992 for leading an attempted coup. The next President pardoned him within two years and, within another four, Chávez had won a Presidential election, on the back of massive support from the poor and the working class. Since then, Chávez had become one of the most recognisable and controversial heads of state in the world, with economic and social transformation at home and aggressive anti-Americanism abroad. Both policies depended on Venezuela's supplies of oil.

'Petrol in Venezuela is so cheap that more than 10 litres can be bought for one bolívar,' said Felix. 'I can fill my four wheel drive for seven *bolívars*.' This was equivalent to just over £2, or the price of a couple of soft drinks.

Chávez's early initiatives had included Plan Bolívar, a programme of road building, housing construction, and mass vaccination. The Orinoco Delta school we visited was a charitable initiative, but there were plenty of other

Seller in Caracas

schools along the river with national government funding, and large posters of Chávez on display in gratitude. Chávez had also overseen the renaming of the nation, by constitutional amendment, to the Bolívarian Republic of Venezuela.

'Now Chávez wants to change the name of our country again – to the Socialist Republic of Venezuela,' said Felix. His tone indicated that he did not approve.

Felix pointed out the building that had previously housed the Hilton Hotel.

'It is no longer the Hilton,' he said. 'The owners were invited to leave by Chávez's government.'

Many American firms had been 'invited to leave' – the Four Seasons Hotel, for example, had been closed. Overall, the USA remained the largest foreign investor in Venezuela (Britain being the second largest). The middle-aged street trader, smoking his cigarette in front of a mobile drinks cabinet designed as a giant Coca-Cola can, seemed to sum up the ambivalence of Venezuelans: love of America, but not the Americans.

Felix parked the car so that we could walk to Plaza Bolívar, where we visited the cathedral (including the Bolívar family chapel, with a modern sculpture of Bolívar mourning his parents and wife). To add to the Bolívar theme park feel, we walked a block to Bolívar's birthplace, now a museum overlooked by the massive glass skyscraper of the Bank of Venezuela.

Plaza Bolívar is not just a series of monuments; it acts as a focal point for pro-government demonstrations. Where were the anti-government demonstrators? we asked.

'We meet in Plaza Altamira,' said Felix.

The idea of opposing parties having their own squares in which to demonstrate was sweet.

Felix also took us to the Panteón National, which contains the tomb of Bolívar as well as tombs and memorials to other famous generals and politicians. An orchestra of young people practised inside, and a military band outside, under the beady eye of a corpulent corporal who was eating a red ice lolly. He was the closest we had seen to a Venezuelan version of Orinoco.

Felix proved to be engaging company as he drove us round one of Caracas' most exclusive areas, Alta Mira, where apartments often sell for the equivalent of $1 million. He had married a woman from the Dominican Republic, who was a regional manager for the Republic's tourism offices in much of Latin America. Meanwhile, Felix was trying to open up new markets for his translation skills by learning other languages such as Japanese.

'I think the best way I have ever spoken Japanese is when I was drunk,' he said, laughing and smiling that large smile.

With his gas-guzzling car and his ambitions to better himself and his family, he was living a Venezuelan version of the American dream. We were sorry to say goodbye to him.

As he drove us to the airport for our flight home, Felix told us that the musicians and the soldiers were practising for the anniversary of Chávez' failed 1992 coup on 4 February. We celebrate Guy Fawkes Night, but he didn't get to be Head of State. As it turned out, Chávez won the referendum and the right to run for President as many times as he wanted.

'We have opened the doors to the future wide open,' he told his followers. But will that future belong to cheap oil to Felix or to the children we saw on the Orinoco?

Whatever the future held for Venezuela, it was time for me to move on to my next location, on a small Scottish island...

TOBERMORY

It isn't every day that you have the chance to try a culinary legend. When you do, it deserves a worthy setting. I'm thinking sunrise over the Pyramids at Giza, or midnight at a café in Montmartre. I didn't expect it to happen to me in Inverbeg.

But then, I didn't know there was a place called Inverbeg. It was the way from Glasgow to Oban, a stop on our connecting drive between flight and ferry. Inverbeg sits by the banks of Loch Lomond. We had time to stop for something to eat, and the Inverbeg Inn was happy to help. The cutlery was on the table in industrial quantities, to ensure fast service, as we picked up the menu and saw…

Scottish cuisine has, it is fair to say, a mixed reputation. Salmon, porridge and kippers all have honourable places at the world food table. The other side of the coin includes haggis and the semi-mythical beast on the Inverbeg Inn menu, as a starter: deep-fried Mars bars.

We had to try them. We had to. An explanatory note on the menu said, 'Yes, we know, but you'll be surprised.'

Helen went to the bar to place the order. We waited. For me, this was the culinary equivalent of those bits of old maps that weren't pink, or any other colour. I have devoted too much of my life to searching for the perfect chocolate fudge cake, but that is more of a pilgrimage. This was exploration.

A young waiter, whose height and spiky blond hair implicated him as the lovechild of a giraffe and a bird of paradise, brought the order. He had a knowing smile. The plate he brought included three items resembling adolescent Shredded Wheat, and a dark, thick dip on the side.

The chef had separated the filling from the rest of the bar and coated it in homemade batter with a touch of coconut. The toffee and chocolate topping had been melted together to make the dip. The effect of all this was to negate one of the prime criticisms of Mars bar haters: that the bars are too sweet. This way, you could have as much or as little of the topping (or dip) as you wanted.

Helen, who would never eat a Mars bar in its classic form, thought these deep-fried bars were an improvement on the standard bar. I have a sweet tooth, which is happy to consume Mars bars, and I thought the coconut was a welcome novelty.

A new recipe for a discredited snack: that was Womble-esque, although Madame Cholet might have uttered the odd *alors* before attempting it.

***

One of the 20th century's abiding legacies is the road trip. The rise of the motorcar led to the creation of a whole new brand of travel, in which you could get in your car and go… anywhere. Some road trips are more famous than others: Route 66; Manali to Leh; the Amalfi coast; the Karakoram Highway. They represent a romantic ideal, using the internal combustion engine to get in touch with your inner nomad.

I've been driven to all kinds of places, and on most occasions I've stayed awake long enough to admire the scenery on the way. I've felt no compulsion to *drive* on holiday. This might have something to do with using the car every other day of the year; a holiday means a holiday

Tobermory

from routine things, like making breakfast or ironing or driving a car. Or it might be based on observation of the more deplorable driving habits in other parts of the world, such as Italians who reverse into the bumper of another car in order to help get out of a parking space, or Parisians who view a pedestrian on a zebra crossing as a target. Whatever the reason, apart from a pleasant drive along the Northumbrian coast, I've been on no road trips or fly-drives, until now, as Helen and I shuffled out of Glasgow airport to pick up a hire car to take us to Tobermory.

As I located the black Volkswagen Golf, sitting in the car park like a neat shiny button, it wasn't love at first sight. The ignition key was a mystery until Helen identified the Swiss Army knife manoeuvre that rendered it useful. The back three of the five doors were impervious to my pleas and threats... they refused to open. To this day, I have no idea who or what may have been in the boot of the Golf as we left Glasgow. They were quiet and well-behaved, which was more than I could say for the car.

The plan was to drive to Oban, catch the ferry to Craignure and then drive up the east coast of Mull to our bed and breakfast cottage. That was another first – my childhood holidays tended to be based in hotels, while Helen's were dominated by trips from south Buckinghamshire to East Anglia, staying in holiday camp chalets where the local ducks were so noisy that you could get your revenge on annoying neighbours by attaching bread rolls to their door. So a B&B was a new experience for us.

I had spoken to the landlady on the phone. She had promised to get her husband to look out for us when we arrived. I wondered if there would be a visitors' book for our comments, and whether we would have to resort to Morecambe and Wise's old coded warnings for those who followed them: 'We shall certainly tell our friends.'

The drive from Glasgow may not qualify as a great road trip. The banks of Loch Lomond were too foggy to be bonny and polite, persistent rain followed us to Oban. Still, it was all going according to plan, until I missed the turning for the ferry terminal. Not to worry: I pulled into the next turning, ready to reverse.

Then the trouble started. I put the Golf into reverse. It lurched forwards. I said nothing; nor did Helen. I found reverse again. The car went forward again, downhill, towards the water's edge.

At this point I thought it useful to consult the diagram on top of the gearstick. What I had assumed was reverse was fifth gear. In a move of astounding design stupidity (what business consultants call 'counter-intuitive'), reverse gear was next to first gear, on the left. I found first gear for the third time. The car went forward, not so fast this time. How could I find the difference between first and reverse before having to perfect my underwater mobile phone technique as I apologised to the hire company?

It is a truth universally acknowledged that men don't read manuals or, if they do, that the text is in Swedish or Japanese. So it was just as well that Helen was there to find the manual, flick through the pages and find that pressing the gearstick down, before moving it to the left, would locate reverse. One three-point turn and a short queue later, we were moving onto the ferry. The captain's gentle Geordie tones soothed us; the only disappointment was not hearing whether there would be a fishie on a little dishie. Within an hour, the Golf was edging onto the island.

* * *

It wasn't Positano, but I liked it. The journey to the B&B involved tiptoeing round some winding residential streets set up the hill from the horseshoe harbour. On the crown of a bend, I stopped the car and gazed down at the distant figures walking from one end of Main Street to the other and the seagulls sitting on the chimneys. After leaving our stuff with the landlady, we went to investigate.

Popular legend – as reported in the Museum of Mull – has it that the fashion for painting the buildings on Main Street in bright colours started with the Mishnish Hotel. The owner was offered a spare tin of paint, so the story goes. Since then, the façade had reverted to black, an uneasy neighbour to Catriona's hair and beauty salon and at a nose-wrinkling distance from the smells of chicken *bhuna* emanating from Sagar's Indian restaurant on the next corner.

We pulled up short from our casual stroll, to inspect Tackle and Books. This was not a pub, despite the name, but a shop offering fishing equipment and books. After my brief experiment with angling on the Orinoco, the rods and nets and baits were not tempting. From now on, in modern management speak, I would be focusing on my core competencies with regard to fish i.e. eating them. As we nosed around, it became clear that Tackle and Books's name was, if anything, underselling it. Art materials sat snug in one corner, facing small furry reproductions of RSPB-branded birds that tweeted and cheeped if you squeezed them. Mobile phones, computer games, printer paper and cartridges also fought for space.

We continued past Tobermory Togs and Toys with its 'What's Rubbish?' board game advertised in the window ('complete with 3D wheelie bin'), and the Island Blue fashion shop, which insisted on identifying itself in purple and yellow. At our next pause, we found an outlet intent on out-tackling Tackle and Books.

Browns Ironmongers Wine and Spirits did not feel it was enough to mix hardware and alcohol. Models of the *Titanic*, sewing and stitching kits, aquarium equipment and goldfish, tennis and table tennis balls, seeds and electric guitars: all consumer life was here. Given the supplies of hammers and ways to get hammered, it was a surprise the store didn't sell anything to do with health and safety. Helen bought an umbrella and tried not to trip over the stock.

'Everything here sells,' said the dark-haired lady behind the counter. 'We try everything and it all sells. That's the thing about being an island, you see: nowhere else to buy the stuff.'

Now protected from the rain, we enjoyed the higgledy-piggledy post office. Not content with the single colour or two-tone exteriors on other buildings, this one sported pink and yellow squares. Tobermory might not be chocolate box, but its post office wanted to be a Battenburg cake.

There were a few tourist traps, but not many unwary tourists. Mull Butchers hadn't attracted eager meat-eaters with its offer of 'freshly shot haggis', or its flashing neon sign advertising 'Organic Free Range Happy Chickens', or the cuddly toy Highland bull wearing a tam-o'-shanter.

Four doors down, past the Macdonald Arms, the art gallery window suggested: 'if closed and you need a painting in an emergency, ring…' I wondered in what circumstances a work of art could resolve an emergency. It would be a cultural solution to our society's problems, if only we could get it on 999: 'police, fire, ambulance or watercolour?'

For further protection from the rain, we stopped at the discount clothes store at the end of the street (prices 'almost as cheap as shoplifting') to buy me a waterproof jacket with a hood. The sun shone for most of the rest of our stay on Mull. But there was a bright shadow hanging over Tobermory: the shadow of *Balamory*.

∗∗∗

'They probably think "F∗∗∗ that"! Or they're probably texting "F∗∗∗ that", anyway.'

It was taking a while to get Donald to relax, but the swearing seemed to help.

'I apologise for the sweary language,' he added, seeing the look on my face. 'I do swear a bit from time to time. I bet you don't ever swear…'

Donald was in the middle of his gallery. He sat in a film director's chair which had his name on it – but on the inside, so nobody could read it if he was sitting there. He was short, stocky, with a full greying beard. His midnight blue shirt had three or four buttons, all undone. The orange toes and heels of his socks set off the blues and blacks of the shirt and jeans.

Donald was an artist who had lived in the area since he was a little boy. A local had suggested we could talk to him about the film he had made about a year in Tobermory and Mull. As we had gone into the gallery, he was selling cards of '*Balamory*' to a dark-haired young couple with two small boys in buggies.

'They came all the way from Northern Ireland just for *Balamory*,' he said when they had gone.

We looked around the array of watercolours of Tobermory and Mull; none too large, none too twee or shocking. If the paintings had been neighbours, they would be just the type you'd want: quiet, courteous, mowing their lawn, keeping an eye out for anyone strange in the close, never making a scene.

'Have we met before?' Donald asked of me.

I recognised the polite challenge, having used it myself the previous week to a pushy new colleague at work. 'Have we met before?' means: '*Who on earth are you?*'

'We're visiting the island. Someone said you'd be interesting to talk to... Sandra.'

'Oh yes, Sandra.' His tone was still guarded.

'She showed us the film you made,' Helen offered.

'Why did she do that? Did she want to put you to sleep?'

He half-laughed, daring us to join in.

We had passed an hour the previous evening watching Donald's film, a sequence of short clips of everything from the quiet dawn to the annual motor rally, from dogs looking at kilt-wearing humans to jellyfish and dolphins in the harbour. There were few faces and little speech, apart from a small child whispering backstage at a pantomime. In its gentle way, the film was Donald's way of redressing what he saw as an imbalance in the world's perception of Tobermory.

'Before *Balamory*, people would come in the gallery and we could discuss gene resequencing or particle dissemination theory or anything. Now it's *Balamory* this and *Balamory* that... it's boring. I wanted the film to be different to the monochrome *Balamory* image we have to the world.'

Although the height of *Balamory*'s fame had passed by the time we got to Mull, it was impossible not to notice its influence. This live action soap opera for small children was filmed in Tobermory, with the producers getting some of the buildings repainted in vibrant colours to represent various characters' houses. A typical episode included Miss Hoolie, the nursery schoolteacher, telling viewers what the weather was like that day; the singing of several songs including *What's the Story in Balamory*; and one character having a problem which others would solve. *Balamory* was going to be called *Tobermory*, until the BBC realised there might be confusion with the Wombles.

'*Balamory* is boring... it just repeats and repeats,' said Donald.

The TV series had brought fame to the village and, in its wake, some reporters who had not endeared themselves to the locals.

'One of them asked me what I thought about the buildings being repainted for *Balamory*,' said Donald. 'I said I wasn't bothered. They were going to repaint them afterwards, so I wasn't bothered. Next thing I know, I'm quoted in the chap's paper "raging" about it.

'Another journalist came up – from *The Times*, I think. He'd been sent into exile or something. He went to a talk and wrote, "The speaker had a Box Brownie and he wasn't afraid to use it!" That's a good line. I think he also wrote something like "Iona is so boring that even the waves pass it by."'

His film about Tobermory had been shown in Inverness, but without the publicity someone had promised him.

'Journalists are lazy, they just copy out the press releases. Is that what journalism is about?'

I assured Donald that I was a writer, not a journalist. But we hadn't got off on the right foot. I asked him if he felt he was an insider or an outsider, or both.

'Is it a problem?'

'No,' I said, I was asking about his perspective as an artist depicting his own village. After a long look and a pause, Donald said that an artist had to be an outsider. Our friendly local had told us: 'Islanders hurt easily.' It was true.

By way of light relief, I wondered aloud what small children living in Tobermory would think of *Balamory*. Would they be confused?

'They probably think "F*** that"! Or they're probably texting "F*** that", anyway.'

This time Donald's laugh was less nervous.

We returned to his film. It seemed odd that he had shown so few faces. One of the amusing clips, at a local concert, showed a small boy crawling around under some chairs in the audience, playing with wellies.

'I didn't want to show faces. That little boy could have grown up to be known as the Boot Boy. I wouldn't want my face on screen. What do faces tell you, anyway? You can tell more about a person by the way they pat their tomatoes at a village show. Look at their fingers.'

It was clear how hard Donald had worked to gain the cooperation and trust of his fellow villagers and islanders. How had he got permission to film backstage at a pantomime, for example?

'I kept expecting to be stopped. I think everyone thought I'd got permission to film from someone else. The level of trust was quite dangerous, in some ways.'

He was already working on a second, longer version of the film, this time with additional footage of local wildlife such as the elusive otter.

'One hour of filming converts into about six seconds of film in the final cut...so I spent the equivalent of 20 whole days working on this...films these days are Bruce Willis and exploding planes, and I've got people watching ripples on walls.'

He laughed again, incredulous. He seemed happy, living next door to the gallery, which it turned out used to be his partner's old surgery.

'I just step through and sell things. I like to chat to people.'

Despite his critical comments about the *Balamory* effect, Donald had noticed a steady stream of visitors from the mainland, coming to Mull to shop.

'I like to watch as people get on the ferry with wheelbarrows and window frames.'

It was time for us to see more of Mull. We bought a painting of Tobermory at sunset, and a copy of the film. As I shook hands with him, Donald was struck by a thought.

'What will you do if people clam up and refuse to talk to you?'

I smiled and reflected on how close Donald had come to doing that. In his polite way, he had reminded me that islanders remain wary of the visitor: the outsider.

***

As we sat in the B&B on Easter Sunday, polishing off the breakfast kippers, we decided to go on a wild duck chase. We'd had a tip-off about a race where we could buy our own numbered plastic duck, and watch it race hundreds of others, which sounded like a lot of fun. We weren't sure where the race took place: somewhere in the south-west, around the Ross of Mull, said our inside information.

The local free sheet had no information on duck races, but our minds were made up. The sun had been shining every day since I'd bought that waterproof jacket. It was a great day for a drive. We pootled down the east coast, slowing for a roundabout in Salen, where a small boy in a T-shirt and short trousers ran out with a bucket, touting for car-washing business. And so we continued towards the island's three castles, facing each other like bickering relatives at a wedding reception.

Torosay Castle is not a castle at all. It's a Victorian mansion built in Scottish Baronial style, completed in 1858. Above the main entrance was a tiger's head, with a dozen deer's heads either side of it on the walls, and additional antlers above each deer's head. A note explained that the tiger was 'Shot by my grandmother in India in 1922'. Adding to the surreal atmosphere was the strong smell of potted hyacinths.

The Guthries, the family who own Torosay, have had many political connections. The family tree was displayed with the caption: 'Being an MP seems to be a hereditary complaint.' In the library there was a portrait of Pamela Harriman – Winston Churchill's daughter-in-law, President Clinton's Ambassador to France and the aunt of the current Laird of Torosay, Chris James.

This was not just a visitor attraction; it was a family home. The library housed some reference books such as the *Dictionary of National Biography*, the *Statistical Accounts of Scotland 1791-9* and various ornithological works, but there was also literature such as *A Passage to India* and the Waverley novels. A sense of self-parodic humour was in evidence from the presence of Dodie Smith's *I Capture the Castle*.

The Castle's hospitality was not of the standard National Trust nature. There were no personal guides, not even in the car park where an NT property can boast an army of pensioners signalling to you every 20 yards 'Please sit down if you wish,' read a notice in the central hall. I wanted to try my hand on the Steinway grand piano in the living room, then English embarrassment won over extroversion and I resisted the temptation.

In the dining room, the fossilised head of an ancient Irish elk above the fireplace stared at us. Another room was dedicated to displays of the Finnish four-masted barque *Viking* in which Chris James's father, David Guthrie James sailed round the world in 1937-8. David's eventful life – including escape from a PoW camp in World War II, polar expeditions and time as a Conservative MP – was featured on *This is Your Life* in 1962. We flicked through the red book used by Eamonn Andrews for that broadcast, and other scrapbooks that gave a glimpse into local life over the past 50 years.

The Castle's Italianate gardens boasted statues imported from Padua; my favourite was the hunting dog delivering its prey to its master. Also on the estate was a farm with highland cattle, cheviot and blackface sheep, and two holiday cottages available to let. Train buffs could get to Torosay by 260mm gauge railway from Craignure, with views of the mainland, including Ben Nevis, on the way.

The second castle, Aros Castle, near Salen, was once the administrative centre of Mull. The castle was in all likelihood built by the MacDougalls of Lorn. For 230 years, from the defeat of King Haakon of Norway at the battle of Largs in 1263, the Western Isles and seaboard formed a semi-autonomous state within the kingdom of Scotland, the Lordship of the Isles. The castle dates from the 13th century, but by the next century it had passed into Macdonald hands. During the Lordship, it was a residence and seat of government of the dominant clan. After the ending of the Lordship (the estates and titles of the Lords of the Isles were forfeited to the Scottish crown in 1493), the castle fell to the Macleans, who in turn were ousted by the Campbell clan. Now Aros perches silent on a small headland, its one main surviving wall overlooking sheer drops down to the Sound of Mull. A few seagulls, and a small boy on a red bike, were our only fellow visitors.

Third and last on our castle-spotting was Duart, which dates back to the 14th century. It is the historic base of the Maclean clan. The first recorded mention of the Macleans of Duart is in a papal dispensation of 1367, which allowed their Chief Lachlan Lubanach Maclean to marry the daughter of the Lord of the Isles, Mary Macdonald. The match is supposed to have been one of true love – though Lachlan helped to persuade Mary's father of his intent by kidnapping him. This incident seems typical of the chequered history of the castle, involving battles for various causes, captures and recaptures and, in the 18th and 19th centuries, ruin.

The Maclean family history says that Sir Fitzroy Maclean (b. 1835), who was brought up in Gibraltar and Malta while his father served with his regiment, saw Duart on a family holiday in the 1870s and decided there and then to buy and restore the castle. So he did. It's not that simple, of course – restoration work continues today. But we saw an Edwardian kitchen and pantry; dungeons where officers of a Spanish Armada galleon were imprisoned; and an exhibition on the Maclean clan at the top of the keep.

The road had narrowed to single track by the time we turned right and made our way through the southern hills of Glen More. A fresh breeze buffeted fluffy white clouds along and ruffled the bright gorse bushes, as sheep nibbled in absentminded fashion at the edges of the track. The car breasted the undulating hills, weaving around an endless sequence of sharp corners, many of them blind. Signs reminded drivers that 'twenty [miles per hour] is plenty'.

Twenty miles per hour might have been plenty for us; it would have been a positive gallop for others who had visited Mull in the past. The most famous visit of all was in the autumn of 1773, from the writer Dr Samuel Johnson and his friend and biographer, the lawyer James Boswell, as part of their tour of Scotland and the Western Islands. According to the latter, Johnson believed that 'by seeing London I have seen as much of life as the world can show'. Despite this extreme Anglocentric confidence, Johnson agreed – after ten years of dithering – to visit Boswell's home country and return before the London law courts resumed business.

Each wrote a book about the trip. Johnson's *Journey to the Western Isles of Scotland* is a lofty and learned disposition on what he found, while Boswell's *Journal of a Tour to the*

Hebrides is at least as interesting for the light it sheds on Johnson as anything about Scotland and the Scots. By the time they got to Mull, the duo had been travelling round Scotland and its islands for two months. Johnson admitted that 'We were now long enough acquainted with hills and heath to have lost the emotion that they once raised, whether pleasing or painful, and had our mind employed only on our own fatigue.' He described the landscape as a 'gloom of desolation' and wondered whether the planting of trees would 'give nature a more cheerful face'. Johnson consoled himself that 'All travel has its advantages. If the passenger visits better countries, he may learn to improve his own, and if fortune carries him to worse, he may learn to enjoy it.' Boswell noted that Johnson 'was out of humour' at times about this 'most dolorous country'.

He had his own worries. Some of the rooms in which the pair stayed were shockingly dirty, he wrote: 'I threw only off my boots and coat and waistcoat, and put on my greatcoat as a nightgown… The mixture of brandy punch at the inn and rum punch here, joined with the comfortless bed, made me rest very poorly.' He wrote to his wife, missing her, and to his father with whom he had been reconciled. Even the parrot in Mrs Maclean's house was a disappointment: 'it could speak very well in Glasgow, but it had rusted in Mull, where the family had now been for seven years'. All in all, while Johnson or Boswell had been more learned and their writings would be famous forever, Helen and I were enjoying Mull more than they did.

Doffing our metaphorical hats to those who had gone before us, we continued our steady progress around the eastern and then the southern coasts, as the sun rose higher in the clear blue sky. We took our time, making regular stops in the little passing bays to avoid delaying others who were in more of a hurry than us. They all raised their hands in polite acknowledgement as they drove past.

Even a seagull took a break from its circling flights to sit on a nearby stone, a smug expression on its face.

The organisers of a fun run at Bunessan had to move their finishing tape to let us through, before we reached Fionnphort, our final destination in the south-west of Mull. We gazed across the water at Iona Abbey, in its perfect setting of yellow gorse, white beach, blue sky and bluer water. Our wild duck chase was over.

***

Whilst we were in Tobermory, the village marked a significant event: the opening of a new Spar supermarket. This was not just any supermarket; it operated from the old Free Church on Main Street. The Spar had been running for some time, and now its owner, local businessman Malcolm, had decided to have an official opening. The church had not been used as a church since World War II, so its reinvention – its resurrection, as the official opening was on Good Friday – was worth celebrating. There was something Womble-esque about finding a new use for an old building.

At this point of our stay, the rain was still about, which caused a logistical problem at the opening. The store staff had set up the obligatory red ribbon for cutting just outside the doors; the rain prompted them to move the ribbon to the entrance itself. Shoppers and visitors had to gyrate under the ribbon in order to enter. Nobody minded. Two small girls in pink tracksuits threw a balloon to each other as the adults unwrapped the cling film and tucked into the *vol au vents* and the quartered Scotch eggs.

Malcolm called on a little old lady – other bystanders told me she had been living on Mull for over 50 years – to cut the ribbon. Despite using what looked like the largest, sharpest pair of scissors since Samson got his hair cut, she needed three attempts to manage it. She did the deed, the shoppers applauded and everyone returned to the Scotch eggs, or went to the mini-café in the corner for soup and a roll. I got a quick word with Malcolm, a stocky man in his fifties with thinning grey hair, a moon face and a worried expression even in his hour of triumph.

'The store's been running for a while, but only at two-thirds capacity,' he told me. 'And the chillers have had a problem or two. But it's all right on the night.'

Malcolm's connection with the building was more than a matter of business.

'My great-grandfather was involved in the construction of the church,' he continued. 'My parents were the last couple to get married in it, too.'

Relatives had used the church as a base from which to sell tweeds, and it then became a gift shop, before Malcolm bought it. He hoped to provide stiff competition for the local Co-op. Malcolm walked away in his smart charcoal shirt and slacks and grey sports jacket to ensure that the little old lady who'd cut the ribbon was photographed being presented with a bouquet. This looked like a last minute remembrance of a task, in keeping with the not-quite-polished nature of the event.

Before leaving the store, I glanced at a couple of shelves of stock – vegetable soup, fruit juice, mustard, mayonnaise – and was surprised to see the labels were in Polish. Perhaps Tobermory was a little more diverse than I had thought.

***

'Yes, but there aren't any jobs for them now. People are moving here from the mainland and getting into social housing ahead of islanders who've been on waiting lists for ages.'

The comment came from a nondescript pensioner, in a suit even older than he was, as Helen and I sat in the chocolate shop-cum-café down by the harbour.

I had picked up a copy of the local community newsletter. It was upbeat from front to back. 'The Ferry

Shop Picks Up Another Award' graced the front cover, alongside photos of younger islanders who had completed commando tests with the Royal Marines Reserves or who had graduated from university.

Mr. Pensionable Suit explained that he used to know someone who had worked on the newsletter, and that it took much consideration to produce.

'You don't print photos of newborn babies – you wait until they're four months old, just to avoid publishing a photo and then having to report a premature death. You don't print obituaries unless it's a family member who's written it, and they've signed a disclaimer.'

The flipside of sensitive islanders was the steps they took to show new residents that they had been accepted. One day on their doorstep, there might be a bunch of flowers – with a mackerel. Another day, if someone had found out that they needed wood for a fire, some chopped-up wood might appear.

That week's edition of the commercially produced newspaper took a contrasting approach to what was newsworthy and fit to print. It led with 'Man dies in crash', opposite 'Waiting lists crisis deepens' and above 'Pipework delayed for Easter'. We pointed out the discrepancy and our elderly informer didn't bat an eyelid.

'Yes, there is bad news. There are drugs on the island now. There was a raid near here a few days ago. But more crime is caused by drink than drugs. We had a gang from Glasgow over here a while ago. They tried to cadge drinks in the local bar and were refused. They went next door, stole a case of whisky from the co-op and then tried to sell it in the pub!'

Ah, yes – the pub. I couldn't leave Tobermory without visiting at least one pub. Anything, or nothing, might happen. A few years ago, while searching for a hostelry in an Irish town, my mother received this gem of advice:

'There are two pubs in this town and, whichever one you go to, you'll wish you'd gone to the other one.'

In the middle of Tobermory's Main Street, the Macdonald Arms would seem, to people used to pub restaurants in most of mainland Britain, like a relic from a past century. How could it run without intrusive background music, quiz machines and a large screen TV? Quite well, it seemed. Without those distractions, you piled into your sausages and mash or curried chicken and – an old-fashioned notion, this – you talked to other people. You could hear what they said. They could hear what you said. The art of conversation was alive and well in the Macdonald Arms.

We told the man at the next table about the unconvincing display in the local butcher's shop window. He smiled.

'I get food delivered once a fortnight from Oban. If you miss ordering on time, you have to go to Oban in person. It's a six hour round trip, but it's free for pensioners like us. It's worth it for the quality of the produce.'

Having enjoyed the strong flavour of the beef in our breakfast sausages, and the kippers we tried another morning, we agreed. Our B&B had been comfortable in every way. I had searched the visitors' book (cover title 'Celtic Hospitality') in vain for any Eric and Ernie-style coded warnings from previous guests, who had come from France, Denmark and Australia, among other places. One had written: 'Please will you adopt me?'

The only odd note as I looked round the Macdonald Arms was the stuffed cat on the mantelpiece. We saw plenty of dogs, but almost no cats, in the village; a local told us that feral cats killed the domesticated varieties. If this was true, the ferals were following in the paw prints of Tobermory's other famous fictional link, apart from the Wombles and *Balamory*. Tobermory is the name of a cat in a short story by Saki which learns how to talk, but embarrasses its human companions with its conversational indiscretions, until it dies in unequal combat with a ginger tomcat.

This allegory did not seem too far from the reality of Tobermory and Mull. On an island of less than 3,000 people, many islanders will know many of the rest, and their business. Bad news travels fast. We found out that two dogs had had to be put down, for killing sheep. 'Those families will be at each other's throats for the next 50 years,' we heard.

Our experience of other harbours had involved cats. Helen and I had sat within inches of the water at Kyrenia in Cyprus, eating local fish while cats surrounded us by the table and on the nearby boats, trying to stare us into donating our dinner to them. Tobermory was different.

As we walked along the harbour one evening, there were no cats. A collie dog rested its front paws over the wall of the front garden of a B&B, as if it wanted to gossip. We weren't in the mood for canine chat: we were seeking out the world's poshest fish and chip van, the only one to have a rating in Les Routiers' directory of fine dining venues.

We found it by the clock tower, standing out in black and silver livery. Two women were serving, one younger and one older, both in standard white tunics and navy baseball caps. We ordered the fish of the day, haddock. The menu had its eccentricities. It was the first time I had come across breaded Tai [sic] fishcake, haggis or white pudding on offer at a fish and chip shop or van.

'The van's been in Tobermory for almost 20 years,' said the older woman as she hunted round for the vinegar. 'We got into the Les Routiers directory by accident. One of the judges for Les Routiers came here on holiday and fancied some fish and chips. He liked it so much he decided to create a special fine dining category just for us!'

That judge knew what he was doing. The firm yet flaky haddock was a pleasure to eat, sitting on the steps under the clock tower, watching the seagulls as the sun went down on another evening in Tobermory. We hadn't met any inventors, but we'd seen plenty of creativity and adaptability. The next stage of the journey would be more dangerous...

BULGARIA

A shrill whistle rang across the path.

'Donald! Stop for a moment,' Millicent called out in her Radio 4 voice. 'We're having a think.'

That was a kind way to describe what was going on in my brain. Thinking might imply looking at an object, a place or a situation, identifying a problem and using your knowledge or experience to reach a conclusion and decide on what to do. In this case, a timid voice in my head was repeatedly squealing:

'I can't do this.'

My left foot was three inches from the edge of the drop. That was the problem. The drop seemed to go on for miles. I tried to look away and ignore the squealing voice. When you tell your brain not to do something, it has a terrible habit of doing it. On most occasions, that isn't a disaster; you get a person's name wrong, or you fail to catch a cricket ball. This time, the squealing voice was echoing around the inside of my skull. Maybe it had escaped and I was speaking aloud; I couldn't tell by now. Sweat was pouring out of the back of my head, drenching my hair, as the mid-morning sun beat down.

I risked a glance up the narrow, winding path at the others, who had stopped to await the outcome. It was too far away to hear what they were saying. *'Didn't he know what he was letting himself in for... I knew those boots were useless... no staying power... why are we waiting?'*

'A little fear is a good thing,' said Millicent. 'I find my threshold goes up slowly over a period of time.'

I didn't want to know about fear or thresholds. I was shrinking back from the edge, trying not to look down at rocks, and rocks, and more rocks. 'Petrified' seemed to sum it up.

In time the sound of footsteps came near. Svetla brushed past as I backed into the rock face behind me. Her round young face was devoid of expression as she dialled a number on her mobile. *Go back, let's go right back, then you can make the call,* I wanted to tell her, but the words stayed in my head.

Svetla finished her call and flipped the mobile shut. She said something about getting the bus to meet us. Then she turned and walked back where we had come, towards the road.

I shuffled along behind her, a few inches at a time, with my left hand clinging to the rocks. The sanctuary of some small bushes, and then the asphalt road, was seconds away. I got there. My hands went to my knees, like a marathon runner at the end of his race, though I had gone only 100 yards at most. Svetla made sure I was all right, told me to wait for the bus and then disappeared back onto the path.

I'd failed, at the first hurdle, and Hell was still to come.

***

Bulgaria had presented a unique problem among the Womble names. The others referred to cities, towns and villages or, in one case, a district. With Bulgaria, there was a sizeable European country from which to choose my destination.

Helen and I had been there in the early 1990s when the Iron Curtain melted away. We'd based ourselves in Borovets, an old skiing resort that had once been a hunting area for Bulgarian Kings. We did meet a King, if you count the one-man band that entertained hotel guests each

Great Uncle Bulgaria... in Bulgaria!

evening in the guise of Elvis. He knew one song, *Love Me Tender*. From the song, he knew one line of the lyrics: 'Love me tender...' Breakfast was a mysterious concoction known as *hameneggz* and the wine label was proud to declare that it was 'Specially selected for Tesco'.

Borovets had been our base for visits to the capital Sofia and other locations around Bulgaria, such as Plovdiv and the Rila Monastery. This time, we decided to try something different. Helen received an email about a walking tour in the Rodopi Mountains, near the southern border with Greece. We'd be walking along traditional shepherds' plains, forest tracks and ancient Roman roads, enjoying the flowers, the birdlife and the remoteness.

The key phrase in the tour literature was the description of the walks as 'for the most part, moderately gentle'. Helen enjoys walking and went to Crete some years ago for a botanical walking tour. My Orinoco-like tendencies had led me to walk, and exercise, less than I should have done, but I was willing to give it a go.

Bulgaria has become a more popular tourist destination in the past 15 years, although you might not have guessed that from our experience at Heathrow on a cloudy Saturday morning. Check-in queues snaked all around us, but only one couple were ahead of us to check-in for Bulgaria Air's flight to Sofia… and another desk opened, just for us.

The man at the Travelex desk had not been asked for Bulgarian *levs* for a while: our modest need for the equivalent of £100 cleaned him out. He couldn't find Bulgaria Air on his computer. Once we had checked in, a browse of the bookshops revealed that the number of guidebooks available on Bulgaria was: zero. I wondered if our flight would touch down to find that Bulgaria had disappeared and been replaced by somewhere else.

The flight was punctual, smooth and under-subscribed. Most rows included one empty seat or more. The woman next to me decanted to Business Class less than an hour after take-off. Great Uncle Bulgaria was the beneficiary, escaping from my hand luggage to bask in the empty seat. The stewardesses didn't offer him any food or drink. On the other hand, they didn't ask him to leave and they didn't ask us to pay for his seat. 'Wombles fly free on Bulgaria Air'… I had the advertising campaign all planned, for a modest consultancy fee.

***

For the first time in many years, Helen and I were travelling in a group. After a sequence of bus tours with multiple stops, we had grown tired of Big Frankie.

Most tour groups have a Big Frankie. On which holiday we first met him, I forget. While Frankie is, no doubt, a good person who loves his mother and serves a useful function in his community, his qualities on holiday are not loveable or useful. As the name implies, Big Frankie takes up undue amounts of space. He has a booming, inexhaustible voice. He uses it to give regular updates on the state of his bowels. He has problems with the concept of time, as it relates to returning to the bus so that the group can continue the journey.

In short, Big Frankie takes a lot of putting up with, and our tolerance had run out some time ago. However, this trip was for a maximum of 14 people, so we took the risk. It was, though, with a little trepidation that Helen and I – with Great Uncle Bulgaria back in storage – walked through Sofia airport, admiring the smart new facilities. We goggled at the posters for strip clubs ('Taboo Club – the most elegant strip club in Sofia', as if there was a strip club elegance league table). And then we were at the exit, meeting fellow travellers and loading luggage onto the minibus for the journey to our one-night stay in Asenovgrad.

Over dinner of salad, lamb kebabs and pancakes, I cast an eye up and down the long wooden table to see who might be a Big Frankie. On my left was Fenella, a retired dressmaker from just south of Edinburgh: snowy hair, parted in the middle, framed a face like a wise wrinkled apple. Fenella brought an air of enthusiasm and gusto to her words and actions.

Fenella was travelling with Annie, one of her daughters. Annie's regular glances at the contents of the bar betrayed her professional roots as a sales executive in the whisky industry. She was due to visit Japan on business soon after returning from Bulgaria.

'Lots of men start telling me how much they know about whisky, so I just tell them I'm on Facebook and they can catch me there', she told me.

Whether this was meant as a pre-emptive strike was not clear; if so, it was wasted, as I don't drink whisky. Annie was short, like her mother, with straight shoulder-length blonde hair. Despite a brisk professional air, Annie was prone to sentimentalism when meeting small domestic animals.

Fenella and Annie had flown from Edinburgh, transferring via Paris – where their luggage had failed to join them on the flight to Sofia. They took it calmly – 'So much simpler not having to unpack on the first night', according to Fenella.

On Annie's left was Millicent, from Canterbury: untidy chestnut curls, broad in the beam, solidly built like other battleaxes. My first impressions of Millicent weren't promising. She seemed fond of emphasising differences of opinion or others' errors, or passing food or drink when others could do it without her help. Her self-appointed role was that of a henpecking wife, correcting her husband Donald or talking about him in the third person, in his presence.

Donald himself was a retired civil service economist, a former resident of Luxembourg and a widower until he met Millicent. Donald was the tallest of us, broad like his wife, grey-haired and bearded. With some hair dye and a wheelchair, he might have passed for the late Michael Flanders.

Anya on his left, on the other hand, was an older Uma Thurman. She had run away from her native Netherlands – 'too many people there' – and was now a vet practising in Durham. Her height, short straight fair hair and ruddy cheeks conspired to give her a tomboy air, despite being in her early fifties.

Beaming away next to Anya was Janet, a teacher whose official retirement date fell during the holiday. She was thin with curly grey hair, a slight twitter to her manner and an exaggeration of tone – as if to show she was listening. Janet, we soon found out, was the resident optimist. Everything was 'super', 'great' or 'lovely', up to and including Armageddon. In the female game of 'no, honestly, I can't eat all that', Janet was an enthusiastic participant.

Simon was the only lone male of the group – though it turned out that he was married – his wife was at home.

Simon was 53, heavily built with thin brown/grey hair, thick studious glasses and a close resemblance to a good friend of ours. Simon had worked at De Beers before retiring aged 50, the lucky blighter.

On Simon's left, Dani defended the honour of Switzerland (though, like Janet, she had married a Dutchman). Dani was in her late 50s with steel-grey short hair and a wiry body. Later in the week, she admitted with some reluctance that she was a psychotherapist. 'I don't tell people because they get very defensive.'

The youngest person at the table was Svetlana, our guide, aged 28, and filling in time while studying her PhD in anthropology. Svetla, as she was known for short, was slim, with fair hair tied back in a ponytail. As the week went on, the more challenging the walks, the shorter Svetla's shorts seemed to get.

There were no obvious Big Frankies. Perhaps things were going to work out better than I'd thought.

***

Not with the walking, they weren't.

The following day, the group visited Chudnite Mostove, which translates as 'Wonderful Bridges' – two natural arch-shaped rock formations. As we climbed each arch in turn, I felt the first faint stirrings of vertigo. Nobody else showed any concern. Donald was far more engrossed in attempting to remember the names of famous Bulgarians. I mentioned Dimitar Berbatov.

'Ah… so he plays for Manchester?'

I avoided explaining the intricacies of City and United. Football was outside what Donald would have described as his milieu.

The question of famous people of different nationalities rumbled on through the week. Dani, representing the provisional wing of the Swiss national tourist board, was not pleased that, for famous Swiss, the group could only think of Mr Lindt and Mr Suchard. I mentioned Roger Federer but, as I had discovered with Donald earlier, sportsmen didn't seem to count in this game.

On the way to our main destination of Yagodina, we walked for a couple of hours around the flank of Mount Kamuka to a small village. No individual element made the walk awkward; it was the combined effect of the stony path, the steepness of the climb at times and the unsettling feeling as you stepped onto any of the thousands of fallen pine cones.

'This is a good little warm-up for the week,' said Fenella, a few paces behind me.

'It's lovely,' Janet agreed.

Helen and I raised our eyebrows at each other. We knew we were novices – me in particular. This didn't sound good.

The next morning, setting out from Yagodina on an asphalt road, we almost agreed with Janet. It was lovely. The sun shone; the trees and crops rustled in the breeze. For company, the group had Jerry, a wayward local hound with a chain tied round his neck, dragging in the dust. Jerry's enthusiasm led him to ignore this impediment as he bounded along, wagging his tail until it seemed certain it would combust.

Then Svetla stopped at a hairpin bend.

'Here we start the walk,' she said, ducking off the road to the right. The group followed her, through some undergrowth... and onto the ledge.

Helen and I were at the back with Millicent. The rest of the group ignored the drop, and the loose stones and chippings on the narrow path. They forged further on, as I came to a halt.

Once that first fatal *I can't do this* gets into your head, it's all but impossible to get it out. To give her credit, Millicent's bossiness from the previous days was now

Yagodina

revealed as a front. She didn't, thank goodness, try to talk me into continuing. There was no coaxing, or patronising. I could have done without the comment about fear, though just hearing another voice helped. A few moments later, Helen and I were back on the road, saved from the ordeal.

The bus arrived and we boarded, numb with humiliation, as the driver took us down more hairpins into the Buinovo Gorge. Svetla's idea was that we would meet the group down in the gorge, once they had negotiated the first stage of the walk. We couldn't face it. Apologising to Svetla, we walked back up along the road from the gorge to Yagodina.

It wasn't 'spectacular', but it was safe. I wouldn't fall off, and there was so little traffic that we weren't going to be run over. One kind gentleman offered us a lift in his Opel. We declined, preferring to walk and thus add a patina of virtue to a dismal day.

***

At that point, we thought we wouldn't be able to look the rest of the group in the face until the bus set off back to Sofia. In fact, considering how irritating they must have found these amateur bumblers, they were all tolerant and supportive. Helen and I did join a couple of group walks in the days that followed; though I spent most of the walking time looking at my feet rather than the views. Janet lent me her stick to help me when the going got steeper and the drops more precipitous. The lunchtime breaks in mountainside meadows, lying among thistles and autumn crocuses and red-winged grasshoppers, enabled me to admire the scenery, bereft of people apart from us.

Millicent and Donald turned back, halfway through one walk, citing knee problems. This gave me some secret, unworthy pleasure; we weren't the only non-completers. Someone once wrote that success is not enough; everyone else must fail. My version would be that it's all right to fail, as long as everyone else doesn't succeed.

There was one other false start. After a walk through the Chairska gorge – including a heroic scramble up a 20 foot rock face – and up through meadows and plum trees, we descended to the village of Trigad to see the Devil's Throat. This is the largest cave in the Balkans. It is also one of several caves to claim itself as the location where Orpheus emerged from the underworld, without his love Eurydice.

It is said that Orpheus, whose fame and success as one of the Argonauts derived from his singing, went into the underworld to persuade Pluto and Persephone to give his dead wife back to him. So tender was his singing that even the ghosts wept, and Eurydice was released on condition that Orpheus did not look at her before they reached the open air. However, he couldn't resist a glance back; and she faded away for the final time.

Standing outside the Devil's Throat, it wasn't easy to conjure this romantic, tragic image of a Greek legend

Bagpipes at the mouth of Hell...

with his beautiful voice and his lyre. The local entertainer who was giving it everything on the Bulgarian bagpipes didn't help. I am not a fan of bagpipes; if I want to hear the sound of a cat being strangled, I'll go and find a cat (and a strangler). Orpheus would not have secured Eurydice's release at all if he'd played the bagpipes.

Millicent, Helen and I didn't make it as far as the 288 steps that led out to the cave's exit. However, for those who believe that the road to hell is paved with good intentions, I can add two pieces of information. First, the start of the road to hell is full of stacks of empty red crates, which once contained bottles of Amstel beer and Coca-Cola. It must be useful to have a choice of beverage when pleading for your dead wife's life with the gods of the underworld. Second, the steps along the road to hell don't have any handrails. For a grade 1 coward like me, that was enough: I was out. Hell hath no health and safety officer.

That was true across the road, too. As we waited for the rest of the group to emerge, I noticed a flimsy zip wire offering brave tourists the chance to fly through the air for a nominal sum. The heavy bandaging on the operator's wrist was a fatal flaw in his sales pitch. Hell, I had concluded, was too dangerous.

***

By opting out of some walks, Helen and I had time to explore Yagodina village. Our hotel (also called Yagodina) sat in the centre. Each morning would bring the sound of bells as villagers led their cows into the surrounding fields. The bells covered a narrow, harmonious musical range – like Cher, without the computer enhancement.

From the balcony of our plain second-floor room, we looked down as owners and cows moved out of Yagodina central to their daily activities. Beyond the cows was the mosque: two storeys, rounded arches, a pile of wood at the front, a minaret with yellow stripes at the top. It only opened for services if at least two people were present in addition to the *imam*. This condition had not been met, it transpired, for years. The call to prayer came on Friday lunchtime. The *imam* sat, hopeful, on the front steps, but nobody responded to the call.

To the left of the hotel was the village's main café, which doubled as a greengrocer's. The family running it seemed to be responsible for looking after up to a dozen children at a time, none older than seven or eight, from various families. The children were well-behaved, although this may have been because they were able to eat anything in the shop. Despite this, none of them showed the slightest trace of obesity: no Orinocos here, just as in Orinoco itself.

The dress code for women depended on age. The over-60s wore headscarves, with roses or other floral patterns, and blue overalls if they were tending their allotments.

Younger women preferred tracksuits, or tracksuit tops with jeans. Along with bursts of *I Want to Break Free*, *Hello* or *Eternal Flame* from the stereo, the tracksuits gave a 1980s flavour to the village.

It was early September, late summer, a time of abundance. The village buildings were functional modern squares, some in turquoise and other pastel shades. The gardens and allotments were bursting with sweetcorn, beans, squash, pumpkins, cabbages and more. In one garden, old tights covered the heads of giant sunflowers to protect the seeds from birds. By the sides of the roads and along the paths going out of Yagodina, apple and plum trees offered their fruit: the plums were small and yellow, like greengages. The smell of woodsmoke was everywhere.

Hospitality came in abundance. Walking past one of the other two cafés in the village, Helen was accosted by an old lady offering her a chocolate from a half-empty box: a strawberry cream. The old lady shared the remains of the contents with other villagers as they walked behind us.

The hotel kitchen baked different varieties of fresh bread each morning, some versions including cheese or rice. The table groaned with homemade yoghurt, strawberry, bilberry and raspberry jams, pine honey and herbal tea from mint fields just outside the village. From a separate table, each group member chose the items they wanted for a packed lunch. Apples, twice as large as fists, vied with outsize tomatoes, as cucumber sticks, cheese and cooked meats caught our attention. The only mass-produced items were chocolate wafer bars, which my sweet tooth appreciated.

The four course evening meals prompted much anguish among the female members of our group. Salads, soups, main courses and desserts or fruit kept coming, despite protestations, including a Womble-esque nettle and rice soup. Towards the end of the week, the hotel took the hint:

we still received just as much food, now with doggy bags in which to store the excess for the morrow.

The cooking was the only manifestation of excess. In other respects, the villagers didn't waste much. Neat piles of chopped wood sat outside every house, ready for the autumn and winter. Cars and vans coasted downhill, switching on the ignition at the last possible moment to save petrol. At night, Yagodina was dark, apart from the mosque and the bright neon sign of the hotel. For the first few evenings, I thought the only night sounds in the village were the 1980s Western pop music blaring out of the hotel restaurant. Then, one night, singing drifted across the square…

***

The mystery of Yagodina nightlife lay up a wooden ladder at the side of a tall white building across the square from the hotel. The group shinned up the ladder and found a way in. The inside was dark. Svetla took us through the second door on the right into a room which, it became clear, was the village library.

The bottom half of the walls were painted blue, the rest white. Only one of the two lights worked. At the far side of the room stood five bookcases, somewhere over half full. Layers of dust indicated that the locals might not have been using the library intensively. We found translations of works by John Fowles and Georges Simenon, Charlie Chaplin's autobiography and a booklet with 'James Bond 007' on the back cover.

On the left, by the window, sat an old manual typewriter and a system of card indexes. By now, a smell of stale cigarette smoke was mingling with the dust. The smoke was coming from the local women whose singing rehearsals we had been invited to join.

There were a dozen in all; the youngest might have been 30 and the oldest over 70, their faces bearing the evidence of years of toil in the fields. The 'traditional'-tracksuit dress code divide was evident again. One of the younger women, a blonde, wore a red tracksuit top over a blouse with a leopard print pattern. When not singing or talking, she smoked; some keys lurked in her hands throughout the evening. If scientists could cross-breed Bet Lynch and Jimmy Savile, this woman might have been the result.

As we sat on wooden chairs and (incongruous in a library) what looked like a park bench, the singers smoked and chatted. Like many music rehearsals the world over, someone had not turned up on time – in this case, the musicians.

After a long 15 minutes, two men arrived. The musical director was a rotund, bald man with a 7 o'clock shadow, a blue baseball cap, a striped top, faded blue jeans and a generous supply of chins. He brandished a red accordion. The soundtrack from the hotel had included, one evening, *What Shall We Do with a Drunken Sailor*? This was the Bulgarian answer: put him in charge of a female choir. His sidekick – a younger, taller, dark haired man – sidled in with a handheld drum and stick.

A discussion ensued, with the musical director attempting to set a running order for the rehearsals. The eventual shrug of his shoulders suggested that some of the choir had strong views on this. He gestured for the session to begin. The women stood in a semicircle, some linking arms while the youngest hooked her thumbs into the pockets of her jeans.

'They're between us and the door,' whispered Simon. 'That's not a good sign.'

The choir's repertoire straddled the boundary between sea shanties and folk songs, if there is such a thing. We weren't sure how many songs they rehearsed, or whether they tried any one number several times; they all sounded the same. As with Yagodina's cows and their bells, the musical range was narrow; as with the cows, it was hard to tell whether some of the singers were enjoying themselves. One or two of them wore the same facial expressions as some of my older relatives after they'd just sat through an episode of *Monty Python* and declared that 'I didn't laugh once.'

Critical opinion among our group split on predictable lines.

'This is super,' said Janet.

'I don't want to be unkind, but I sing in a choir,' countered Anya. 'And they're very enthusiastic, but... some of them have better voices than others.'

At dinner the previous evening, Anya had given us a colourful version of the story of Elijah as portrayed in the *Oratorio*, as performed by her choir. Folk shanties might not have been to her taste, but, as Simon had observed, our exit was blocked, so there was no chance of sneaking out. A few local men, whom I took to be sons, boyfriends or husbands, sauntered into the room to watch.

'Well, I think we should perform something for them,' declared Millicent.

Donald and Millicent were keen members of their local amateur dramatics group in Canterbury. What did Millicent have in mind?

'Something they'll enjoy... something simple to teach. It's a piece of cultural exchange,' she said in a voice brooking no argument.

By this stage, the singers had turned their semicircle into a full circle – quite a feat in the small space available – and were moving clockwise in time to their latest number. Before our hosts knew what had hit them, Millicent, Donald, Svetla, Anya and Janet pushed their genteel way into the circle, held hands with their neighbours and joined in the dance. The Bulgarians didn't take it amiss; they just carried on as if nothing had happened. At the end of the enhanced dance, Millicent leaned over to Svetla and stated:

'We'd be very pleased to teach these ladies the hokey-cokey.'

'That is a dance?' asked Svetla.

Millicent nodded and smiled. We waited while Svetla translated this offer, wondering what the Bulgarian words were for 'hokey-cokey' or for other useful phrases such as 'cultural imperialism' or 'just humour them, they're leaving at the end of the week'.

'They would like to try your... hokey-cokey,' said Svetla, after an age.

And so a group of middle-aged, middle-class Britons got its chance to leave a lasting cultural legacy in southern Bulgaria. The hokey-cokey never featured in the film footage I had seen of space shuttles, bound for distant galaxies, sending aliens examples of the best human art, music and science. To be fair to Millicent, anything more complicated would have been impossible to teach in such a short time. So my dream of seeing Bulgarians performing the minuet, as per the Wombles' *Minuetto Allegretto*, didn't have a chance.

Millicent took the lead to begin with, gesturing for our hosts to move towards the centre of the circle and then move out again. As the singing reached 'That's *what* it's all about', she wagged her finger at all and sundry. The trouble was that – as far as Donald was concerned – that wasn't what it was all about.

'You're teaching it wrong,' he told his wife. 'You need to add the *knees bend, arms up, ra-ra-ra.*'

The Bulgarian women were enjoying their impromptu dance lesson, giggling and gossiping to each other. They continued to hokey-cokey, under Donald's instruction, with the addition of bended knees, arms going up towards the ceiling and some *ra-ra-ra*. One of the younger men – a boyfriend or possibly son of one of the women – joined in.

Satisfied by the results of his tuition, Donald retreated out of the circle to take photos on his iPhone. I'm not sure how good the results were. It was a tight space in which to dance, let alone take photos, and the enthusiasm of the Bulgarians outweighed their dancing skill on the whole, so it was a poky, ropey hokey-cokey.

After a few minutes of this, the youngest woman in the circle retrieved a decorative metal belt and started a spot of faux belly-dancing, to much clapping and cheering from her colleagues. The session adjourned to the pub where the circle would be performing the following night.

Millicent asked me: 'Wasn't that good?'

I racked my brains for a diplomatic reply: 'I've never seen anything like it.'

***

I wandered through my home village a week later, ducking the branches of the copper beech trees and picking the blackberries. The steepest drops from which I could fall here were the kerbs of the pavements. Rupert Brooke was right, I reflected as I dodged the start-of-term school run; there would now be some corner of a Bulgarian field that was forever doing the hokey-cokey.

The self-sufficiency of the villagers would ensure that there was honey still, for breakfast rather than tea. It had been a strange week, in a beautiful place with hidden dangers. Yagodina isn't a rural idyll – it may be romantic in high summer, but its geographical isolation may mean it's less than perfect in a cold winter. The villagers looked healthy enough on their home-made cheeses, bread, fruit and tea; their favourite import seemed to be the cigarettes they smoked while taking a rest from picking potatoes or chopping wood.

My memory meandered back to a lively discussion on one of the group walks, about salvaging things from skips.

'I found an ironing board in the woods near my house once,' Anya had claimed. 'I took it to the charity shop. There's always a skip nearby. Students dump their old clothes in it, so I wash the clothes and take them to the shop, too.'

Annie had replied that she saw a fridge standing by a skip.

'It had a note on the door saying "WORKS BUT NEEDS CLEANING". I took it home and painted it green to match my kitchen. It lasted six years until the door fell off.'

As we had negotiated the thickening forest and the fallen pine cones, I'd wondered how long it would take for this positive attitude to recycling to become the norm, back home. Little did I know that, for some people, the example set by the Wombles had influenced their lives and even their careers…

CHILDREN OF ORINOCO

'Hello,' said the woman with white hair and the slightly spangled blouse with pink daisies. 'Can we help you?'

'I was wondering if Hughie was around.'

'He isn't around at the moment.'

'Are you expecting him?'

'We're always expecting Hughie!'

Perhaps I should have confirmed the appointment.

'Come on through. Would you like a cup of tea?'

'Well,' I said, ready for this moment, 'I've actually brought some stuff for you.'

We wandered back into the car park. I opened the boot of the Mini to show my hostess the boxes of bathroom and kitchen tiles that I had brought as a gift. They were reminders of past redecorations and, until today, resident in the garage.

'Oh, those will be lovely,' she said. 'But they look heavy. I'll get a trolley.'

She returned a minute later with an escapee from a supermarket chain. Once we had loaded it, we wheeled it into the hall, through a connecting corridor and into a room filled to the brim with shelves, blue crates and piles of what could only be described as stuff: coloured foil off-cuts, sponges, sticky foam shapes, yarn. One handmade banner hung from the ceiling, declaring 'Play' in blue, while another read 'Create' in pink.

My hostess found me a cup of tea and a seat and explained it all while we waited for Hughie. Her name was Glenda. Being retired, she worked three days a week for the Oxfordshire Scrapstore in which we sat, in the Bullingdon Community Centre, on the outskirts of Oxford. The Scrapstore had an alter ego – Orinoco – to reflect its activities in collecting and reusing paint, scrap materials or tools from individuals and businesses. There were two main markets: encouraging people to use scrap for domestic purposes, and finding potential art materials for children and schools. Or, as they put it, 'banishing boredom and saving the world.'

My first impressions had not been hopeful. I had been expecting a crowded car park; there was one other vehicle. Maybe people preferred being bored to saving the world.

The main entrance had peeling tangerine paint and an array of notices. A door on the right was open, leading to the main hall, from which voices were coming. In the hall were a couple, fighting losing battles with middle age and with jumble splayed across lines of trestle tables. The man sported a receding grey hairline, a neat pointed beard and a sweater with turquoise hoops. This didn't look much like the salvation of the planet.

I had arranged to meet the Chief Executive Officer, Hughie, who didn't seem to be around. Glenda was more than happy to fill in for him, with her genteel, polished sales pitch. She was pleased with the store's latest major haul, from a local warehouse operator with three lorry loads of material to dump. There it was (or some of it, anyway) in the corner: bright red cushions, beach bags, handbags, necklaces and picture frames.

'It would all have gone in the tip,' said Glenda. 'Now we can sell it on for £2 a cushion. The money's a great help with the rent for this place and the van.'

She paused to greet regular customers and to advise a short woman in a tracksuit on the likely location of a six-inch distemper brush.

'Look at all this paint we buy in…we sell it for £2 a time to non-members, so we don't undercut the local shops, but £1 to members…These books fetch up to £2.50, people use them for diaries or colouring books or various things…'

It turned out that membership of Orinoco cost £10 a year, for which I would enjoy discounts on a wide variety of items, with £10 worth of scrap thrown in.

'Here's some wallpaper we bought from another scrapstore in Swindon. We often sell it to schools for their plays. These sheets of plastic make very good decoration for carnival floats…'

Glenda brandished a small, thimble-like object at me.

'These are very popular. They're the bottoms of walking sticks. We encourage people to use them as stamps, for creating artwork.'

Her next exhibit was furry and cylindrical.

'That looks like a paint roller,' I said.

'It is. But it could be very useful as a cat scratcher.'

Tobermory would be proud – new uses for old objects. I looked up at the top shelf in front of us, to see a dozen big boxes with a forgettable brand of roller skates. Glenda admitted that they had been in stock for some time. Clearly there were limits to the ingenious reuse of refuse. We squeezed round to the far corner of the store to find more pots of paint than anyone could ever hope to see.

'We got these from a painter and decorator,' explained Glenda, 'or from his solicitor, rather. He was dead, you see… anyway the solicitor didn't know how to dispose of it all, and he asked us if we would take it. Of course, we said, "yes, please"…but it's taking a long time to sort it out. We thought it would be good stuff, but it wasn't.'

That explained the semi-congealed evidence on the sides of the paint pots. The contents had to be mixed with sawdust to enable them to harden, after which the tips would accept the hardened paint. Otherwise, tips normally directed unwanted paint to Orinoco. In an ironic reversal of the normal cliché, it seemed that the paint pots were painting themselves out of their own corner, taking up more and more space in the store.

We edged away from the paint, and I was admiring a collection of Connect-o-Mecc (a version of Meccano) when Hughie groaned into view.

'I'm sorry, I forgot about our meeting completely,' he said. 'I went for 'a drink' with a friend last night. Without others to constrain us…I didn't get to bed until 6.30am. I've got a three-year-old daughter, I can't do this any more!'

Hughie had been, at various points in his career, a presenter of a well-known TV wildlife series and a theatre performer. He was tall and stockily built, with bloodshot eyes and small spectacles, and a green printed Cape Range National Park T-shirt.

'I'll just get a notice printed for the Swap Shop, and then we can talk.'

The Swap Shop, a regular event to which all comers brought their unwanted goods and collected anything desirable they found, was starting in less than half an hour. Hughie printed his notice, sobered up, and we talked.

Orinoco, Hughie explained, had been running for many years, and using the Orinoco name for at least ten years before the advent of the 'new Wombles' on TV in the late 1990s. But lottery money ran out and so, it appeared, did Orinoco's luck. It moved to the Community Centre in 1999 and stayed in a state of disrepair for several years, until Hughie came along. He took up the story with the air of someone who has dealt with the same enquiry many times and has pared his responses to suit.

'After my baby girl was born, I went to postnatal classes with my wife, and thought that art wasn't being taught very well for small children. Then I heard a radio ad for Orinoco and came along. At that point, the whole operation was only open to members, it had no stock and it never opened. It owed a lot of money. My brilliant diagnosis as consultant was to open it up to all comers, to get stock from local businesses and to start opening again! I sat here on my own for the first few events, and people still came. They'd been turning up even in the days when Orinoco was closed, just in case it wasn't.'

He broke off to tell everyone in earshot that 'The Swap Shop is now open'. I followed him through to the hall, where a respectable collection of visitors were already bringing in their wares and jostling each other to check what else had been brought.

'There are over 800 members now,' said Hughie, as he gyrated to a blues record like Baloo from *The Jungle Book*. 'And we have 1500 people on our mailing list. We didn't have any marketing budget when we re-opened in 2006, so that meant a lot of e-marketing.'

He was frowning as he surveyed the scene. It was busy, I suggested.

'Well, this is actually quite quiet for a Swap Shop. We usually get 300 people a day, and we shift a ton of stuff... and I mean a ton. It's all weighed, you know. Look at these boxes of books behind us. I build these stocks up and we shift up to 2,000 books a year.'

Clothes, games, jigsaws, books, records, bathroom scales, CD holders, videos, cassette tapes, fax machines, computers, an old Hoover, a banana stand – all manner of consumer goods were available. I wondered if Hughie had ever refused to display or sell any item brought in.

'Well, there was a set of illustrated copies of the *Kama Sutra*...we do get some strange things. On the very first occasion I ran these events, a little old lady came in, left one item and went out again. She didn't say a word. The item was a pearl necklace and we never saw her again.'

Hughie looked on as the visitors continued to jostle, bring and take away their wares; children, parents, grandparents all joined in. A little girl with Shirley Temple curls dashed out of a Wendy house and between Hughie's legs.

'It's marvellous,' he said, half to himself. 'We encourage the reuse of resources and we embed ourselves in the community. And we have revived the community – we more or less run this centre. The Swap Shops are an excellent PR exercise. And we run other events as well.'

Beneath the faux management-speak, he did seem proud of Orinoco. But the name itself was not his doing.

'Of course it's an excellent name. But I could have rebranded the whole operation. Orinoco had come to be a byword for poor service, no service. In the end, we kept it. But we used to have a Womble in the logo, and Womble pictures around the place, and I've got rid of all those. Still, things have worked out. It's even a kind of sub-economy we're creating. Some of what people collect here today will be in a car boot sale tomorrow.'

I shook Hughie's hand in thanks and went to look at the book section. *Alien Nation*, *The Canadian Student Employment Guide*, Agatha Christie and Sue Townsend competed for attention. A copy of a book which had gone AWOL from my shelves appeared in the middle of the pile. I tried not to snatch at it.

After a short break for a sugary doughnut, I left... or tried to leave. The car park was now full to bursting, blocking the Mini in. One of the culprits was Orinoco's vivid red van. A few apologies and laboured manoeuvres later, the blockage had cleared. I sped away, perhaps a little wiser, in a Mini hundreds of tiles lighter and a few books heavier.

***

Santa sat in the window, clutching a half-empty bottle of cognac. He didn't seem in a hurry to get on with his delivery schedule. Maybe the cognac was warming him up against the December chill in the air. Or maybe this was a glimpse into a future where the arrival of Santa, and the contents of his sack, would be less important; a world where Gail's ideas had moved from the fringe to the mainstream.

I'd first made contact with Gail some months previously, via her website. 'Welcome to the Womble Burrow,' said the homepage, next to a group photo of the seven Wombles from the original TV series. At the top of the page were links to seven sections, each with a different Womble head as the link. I tried a few. The Fashion page linked to galleries of Wombles in attire following various fashion themes, with a hippy Womble, a Santa Womble and even a version of Easy Rider, or Easy Wombler as the caption called it. The travel page featured photos of Wombles posed by some of the world's best-known locations such as the Eiffel Tower, the Atomium, the Grand Canyon, the London Eye and Houses of Parliament. I was already beginning to feel overwhelmed, in the same way as you do after walking through the Louvre or the palace at Versailles. That was before I reached the recipes page and its handy tips for Tomsk's tofu salad and Tobermory's tomato soup.

The merchandising page confirmed my suspicions. 'Here, for your nostalgia-festive delight, is my Wombles memorabilia collection. It is not for sale!' There were (among other things) jigsaw models, *papier mâché* sets, badges, magnets, puppets, books, T-shirts, jumpers, leggings, socks, slippers, ties, dinner sets, cake decorations, lampshades, duvets, curtains, card games, arcade games, key rings, hairgrips, carrier bags, backpacks, CDs, LPs, DVDs, videos, soft toys, pyjama cases, writing pads, pencil cases, postcards, soap, toothbrushes and mirror and hairbrush sets. In the light of the evidence, I felt it was reasonable to conclude that the website owner was a Wombles obsessive.

Yet that was not the whole story. From the site homepage I followed the other main link, to a site devoted to 'sustainable consumption research to develop low-carbon lifestyles'. This was no ordinary obsessive, but a university research fellow who had written articles and books with intimidating titles such as *Consuming Values and Contested Cultures* and *Grassroots Innovations for Sustainable Development: towards a new research and policy agenda.*

What was the connection between an old TV series for children and this academic work? Was there a connection? I had to find out. That was how, one Saturday in December, I found myself hovering around the edges of an art gallery on a university campus in Norwich.

I spotted a short woman, probably in her late 30s, with shoulder-length straight brown hair which was parted at the centre. She was wearing fashionably geeky spectacles, a chocolate brown top and black trousers. This was Gail, Wombles lover and pioneering social scientist. We introduced ourselves, bought hot chocolates from the gallery café and sat down for a chat. It quickly became clear that the Wombles had been a part of Gail's life since the original TV series.

'One of my earliest memories is of watching *Star Trek* – the original, of course. I was only 3 or 4 and I guess this was around the time the Wombles started to be on TV, around 1973 or 1974... there was this abiding feeling from the middle of the 70s about the Wombles and about being charmed by the Wombles. And it kind of fitted in with a couple of other things that were around at the time and reinforced each other.

'One was *Blue Peter* – not necessarily the pets and exploits and charity appeals, but "here's one I made earlier" – making things out of toilet tubes and sticky back plastic. That struck a chord with me. I made Christmas presents out of felt and sticky-back plastic and washing up liquid bottles and that seemed like a perfectly nice thing to do. You're giving someone something you've made and put your own energy and thought into. It reinforced the

Wombles' approach to recycling and making things. But it wasn't a mad obsession at that time.'

So far, so idyllic as far as a late 20th century English childhood went, until Gail realised her passions were not supposed to survive into adulthood.

'I started to get comments such as "isn't it time to move on from the homemade presents?" It's acceptable for a 10 year old to do it, but once you reach a certain age you should move on – the real world isn't about making good use of old rubbish. That was the sentiment. I thought it was absolutely outrageous. How dare you, I thought?'

Gail's voice, and her stare, hardened. Even at 25 years' distance, the memory rankled.

'It was very hurtful to be told that someone close to me would prefer me to go to a shop and spend some money on something thoughtless which would probably end up in landfill… that stuck with me. I kept making things, but I stopped giving the presents to people who didn't appreciate it. I thought it was that attitude in society which was deficient rather than the fact that I'd kept my *Blue Peter*/Wombles ethos.'

Meanwhile, although the Wombles were no longer on TV, a teenage Gail rediscovered them through the music of Mike Batt.

'I came back to it as a teenager, probably around 14 or 15 – by digging out the records… I played them for a laugh and realised these are really good songs… fantastically charming – very funny lyrics and touching and moving and simple. The characterisations came through the lyrics and they were fantastic pastiches. These aren't just throwaway, *Bob the Builder*-type songs. So, although it's deeply uncool and always has been, I genuinely appreciated the music as an adult rather than as a child.'

Having whiled away the car journey to Norwich with *The Very Best of the Wombles*, some of those lyrics were fresh in my mind. As Gail talked, I savoured the mental images of a Womble astronaut eating cucumber sandwiches (*Womble of the Universe*) and a Womble spy in James Bond style, complete with a false moustache and a bottle of invisible ink (*To Wimbledon with Love*).

In the 1980s and early 1990s, Gail's collection of Womble memorabilia grew, partly through her own efforts and partly through friends who scoured charity shops and car boot sales for her. And then…

'And then about 10 years ago I signed up to eBay and that was fantastic. It was like being in the biggest charity shop or car boot sale in the world! Then my collection exploded enormously as I could get hold of all sorts of memorabilia that I'd never come across. Also, in 1998 the Wombles were relaunched with a new TV series. Suddenly there was new memorabilia that I could buy and I bought everything I came across in the shops. So the collection of stuff exploded in terms of size and comprehensiveness. The crazy thing is, even ten years later there are still things that come up on eBay from the original merchandise that I never knew existed and that's absolutely extraordinary. Where has it been hiding all this time?'

By this time Gail was living with her partner, five years older than her. It seemed that sharing Gail's life with a collection of fictional furry creatures did not put him off.

'My other half had always known I was a Wombles enthusiast and I think I gradually won him round. He certainly didn't mind when the house became overgrown with toys and pictures and lampshades and all the rest of it. But it did get a bit much after a while. So now it's all in boxes in the loft. It starts to feel like you're living in a theme park!'

Fans of a TV series often identify with one or more of the characters. I wondered which Womble was most similar to Gail's own personality.

'I always had a soft spot for Wellington because he's brainy and a scientist. He always seems to have an openhearted approach. Wellington is humbly surprised by the wonder of the world... an open-minded learner trying things out – not like Tobermory, who's a bit of a 'bish, bash, bosh' geezer. There weren't any female younger Wombles to identify with in the original series... and who wants to identify with a clichéd female stereotype, cooking and cleaning and doing all the washing for the male members of the household?'

I had never thought of Madame Cholet in such a traditional light. Gail continued her story.

'Around the age of 12-13 I began to get interested in Friends of the Earth and Greenpeace and the environmental movement and the peace movement... When I was at school, I was always very good at science and I anticipated going to university and doing chemistry or something like that. But my interest in social and environmental movements grew and I realised that being a scientist and coming up with technical answers wasn't going to help the world... we need to understand how the world works and come up with social solutions. So I ended up doing a social science degree, which was a bit of a shock to the system..., then a Masters in Environmental Science looking at the social side. Now I'm looking at community-based initiatives for a greener lifestyle or to transform society.'

So this was it. Beneath the soft-spoken, personable exterior of a Wombles fan lurked the scientist who wanted to change the world.

'You could see sustainable consumption as just a bit of green consumerism where we buy one brand of washing powder instead of another because it's more environmentally friendly, and I find that a very weak answer. Society's problems are much deeper rooted and go to our systems of provision, so we need to change those systems... using local food systems, farmers' markets, bypassing supermarkets, using local currency systems which promote different types of behaviour.

We consume things to survive, then to make us feel happy – broadly speaking – to express identity, to belong to a group etc. The challenge is to say that beyond the basic necessities, can we achieve well-being without consuming things? Plenty of people are demonstrating ways of doing so in a way without consuming stuff to do it. We can achieve social and psychological well-being without consuming stuff.'

Before the conversation drifted into the deep waters of academic jargon, I asked Gail to give me some examples.

'Take lawnmowers,' she replied. 'Lawnmowers, power tools, stepladders, general garage equipment – we all buy our own and they sit and gather dust for 99% of their lives. A neighbourhood or village repository is a way for people to share them – one lawnmower for 50 houses.

'Another example might be an eco-village which makes a deliberate decision to forego certain types of material consumption. You find that people in those places have levels of well-being at least as high as people who live a regular lifestyle – a shared purpose with others. Those types of activities that are not materially based deliver the well-being and social esteem. We need to feel we are useful and to have a purpose.'

I wondered how the big corporations would feel about their purpose in this brave new world. For the first time, Gail didn't seem to have a ready-made answer.

'I've never thought about it from Tesco's point of view… but any successful business needs to be able to respond and adapt to changing circumstances… There will be new markets opening delivering new types of services. I imagine less of our economy will be based on importing and retailing and disposal cheap plastic and more will be based on service-rich social networking. That still needs organisations to coordinate it.'

It dawned on me that, in a cynical world, I was talking to the ultimate optimist – someone who believes she can change the world. This seemed to give Gail pause for thought.

'I suppose I am… I don't necessarily believe that the alternative models will become mainstream in my lifetime. The important thing is to show there is another way and to move in that direction. Pockets of people are showing we can do things differently. There have always been cooperatives, communes, collectives. I like to celebrate them for their difference.

'Even in the last 20 years there have been massive changes. If you talked about recycling back then, you were considered a freak. The main thing is to keep a beacon of hope alive that things can be different.'

So would it be possible, in the future, to live like a Womble?

'Well…' Gail considered. 'They live in a burrow, which is an earth-sheltered house, presumably with low energy consumption, local food from foraging. They've got all their resources locally. If you transpose that now to experimental builders, architects, communities, they're all looking for technological and social innovation to move towards more sustainable societies.'

She took off her glasses and I could see that her eyes had lit up with enthusiasm.

'When I was in the US, we went to see some experimental low energy houses called earthships – basically Womble burrows – which don't require any utility connections. They collect all their own water from the roof and generate their own electricity. They maintain a stable temperature regardless of the external climate. So a house doesn't require external water input in the desert. It's banked up with earth on three sides with a fourth side of glass facing the sun.

'It's quite extraordinary. We stayed in an earthship for two or three days. It felt extraordinary to be completely self-sufficient. Your house would protect you by virtue of its own design rather than by external inputs. It was very transformative. I thought – wow, I'd love to live in a house like this… I thought it would be a great way to live.'

Gail fell into a reverie. I looked at the woman opposite me in the café. Beneath the science and the jargon and the ideology was the dream of a child for a better world, which could, one day, come true. I didn't know whether to be touched or scared.

I introduced Gail to Orinoco. She pressed his paw and showed no embarrassment as *Remember You're a Womble* blasted across the café. We said goodbye and I watched her get on her bike, carefully parked outside the gallery, and slowly cycle away.

The next day, I thought of Gail as I looked at the recumbent Santa in the post office window in Halesworth high street. It was the first Sunday in December, but this was a seasonal Suffolk high street with a difference.

The second-hand bookshop should have been a good bet for some bargains. It was closed. A sign in the window listed this year's typical Christmas presents as 'Nike trainers, iPod, PlayStation…' and described their cost as 'too much'. I felt Gail would agree with the sentiment.

Then there was Santa. Perhaps his delivery schedule had driven him to drink, or he had tried and failed to use the red mobility scooter that sat on the pavement. Whatever the reason, the post office was shut and Santa was going nowhere.

Other shops were closed, too, though CA Palmer & Son Butchers (est. 1967) seemed to be under renovation, with burly men dashing in and out of it carrying hammers and other tools. The oak front door of Lewis Furniture remained resolutely shut. I admired the herringbone brickwork above the multi-coloured fascia and window display of Halesworth Toy Shop. The street was close to empty and silence reigned, apart from the quacking of ducks in a nearby stream.

I paused to look at the shop signs, many in old-fashioned capital letters or decorative typefaces. Some signs had telephone numbers, but there were no email addresses and no mentions of websites. Then I realised something else was missing. I'd walked all the way down an English high street without seeing a single national chain or big supermarket.

It turned out that Halesworth was in the middle of the 'Cranbrook Triangle', an area of about 40 miles in East Suffolk without a single Tesco, Sainsbury, Asda, Morrisons or Waitrose store. Was this a preview of Gail's brave new world of local community self-sufficiency, or just a glimpse into a past that would soon disappear?

***

The brass band segued from *Land of Hope and Glory* into *Dancing Queen*. This wasn't a comment on the social skills of our monarch, I was sure; more a sign of what Dirk Gently called the fundamental interconnectedness of all things. Dancing Queen, after all, was one of ABBA's most famous hits. ABBA came to fame by winning the 1974 Eurovision Song Contest. Each year, the contest features an interval act to keep the audience awake while the votes are counted; in 1974, the interval act was… the Wombles. And just to top things off, in 1974 the venue was Brighton, and here we were, 35 years later, up the road in Hastings.

On the other hand, if everything did fit together like that, things might be boring. You need the element of surprise, which was where Clive came in. Clive was a guerrilla and he'd agreed to meet Helen and me for Sunday tea, in Alexandra Park.

I was out of breath from half-walking, half-running to the park café. Our schedule had been disrupted before we left – a relative of Helen had locked themselves out of their own house. I'd managed to break in via a side window and my version of the Fosbury Flop, and that had used up most of my energy for the day before we got within 100 miles of Hastings. Too late, I remembered that I hadn't sent Clive a photo of Helen or me. How would he recognise us?

'Neil! Hello, there you are!'

I whirled round to see Clive sitting on a rock just outside the café.

'Hi, Clive. You managed to recognise us, then?'

He smiled and pointed at the small Womble I was holding.

'Ah… yes.'

We shook hands and waited for a table at the café to become available. A couple of minutes later, Helen and I were walking up the ramp to the table, while Clive clambered through the railings that separated the café from the surrounding area.

Clive was of medium height and build, with blue eyes and short whitish-blond hair brushed back from the forehead. He wore a grey-green shirt over a black T-shirt and black jeans. Throughout our conversation, he smiled; his voice had a quality of surprise and excitement, as if someone had just given him his best Christmas and birthday presents, ever.

When I returned from the café with our drinks (Orangina for Clive, tea for Helen, hot chocolate for me), Clive was admiring Orinoco.

'He's wicked!' he said, in a soft spoken accent that was hard to place. 'What else does he sing?'

I confirmed that Orinoco had but one song in his repertoire.

'That's a shame. I remember the Wombles and picking up litter. They had a house made of old newspapers, didn't they? That was good – reusing old stuff.'

Clive had watched the original Wombles TV series as a small boy – in his case with his older brother Dave, but they took their enthusiasm further than I ever had.

'Dave got into punk when we were kids, and our bedroom got covered in things from *NME, Smash Hits,* all those magazines. Dave took the wallpaper off and put that stuff up instead – just like the Wombles' house. Our parents weren't too happy!'

He liked the music too. 'Somewhere or other I've got a copy of the *Mike Samms Singers Sing Wombles Greatest Hits.* My dad bought a record player and that set me off... punk, reggae, the Wombles, everything. I reckon if you listen to *Remember You're a Womble* there's a bit of a reggae thing going on there.'

I'd asked to meet Clive because of his gardening.

'I got into gardening because of my granddad's garden,' explained Clive. 'All those vegetables in little rows. And I liked his neighbour's garden, which had a pond with goldfish. I loved *The Wombles* and *Blue Peter* with all that gardening and recycling and environment stuff.

'I've always had this feeling in me. I joined the RSPB when I was 12, because I saw a friend throwing stones at birds' nests. I've always been a bit of a campaigner... I was there with the Twyford Down protestors.'

And that was the key, because Clive wasn't just a common or garden... gardener. He was a campaigner: a guerrilla gardener. Guerrilla gardeners target an abandoned piece of land that they don't own to grow crops or plants, in order to reclaim land from what they see as neglect or misuse and to assign a new purpose to it. Some guerrilla gardeners carry out their actions at night, in relative secrecy, to sow and tend a new vegetable patch or flower garden. Others work more openly, seeking to engage with members of the local community. The term 'guerrilla gardening' is believed to have been first used in the early 1970s.

'I got into guerrilla gardening when I read about it a few years ago,' said Clive, his eyes lighting up. 'I started finding spaces, and planting fruit trees or sowing seeds.

I usually do apples and pears because they're easiest, and they fruit quickly. I survey an area and see if it could do with a tree! I used to do vegetables, too, but that's more work – all the watering and weeding, you have to keep going back.'

So, I asked, was Clive a night-time guerrilla?

'I started out at night, yes, but now I do it during the daytime as well.'

Had he ever been caught in *flagrante nasturtium*?

'Well, I ran into a policeman one night while I was planting. He was very polite; asked me what I thought I was doing. "Ah, you're one of that lot," he said when I explained. "We could do with more of your type around."

'And I do get some stick sometimes. Tony from up my road found me planting vegetables in his garden at 2a.m. one morning. I told him I wouldn't have to do it if he looked after his garden like he should. Now he's growing beetroot and other stuff, so it looks like the message got through! But mostly people don't mind what I do. I'm adding, not taking away: it's a win-win situation. I even got asked to do some gardening work once by someone when they found out about the guerrilla stuff. That's not why I do it, but it was nice to get that reaction.'

So why did he do it?

'It's good for the environment, and it's fun! And once the fruit trees bear fruit, I can help myself and so can other people. There's no committee, no logistics, I don't have to ask permission. I'm not the only one - I've found about nine other guerrilla gardeners in the area. It's great to know you're not alone.

'I'm not sure how many trees I plant in any given month. A decent tree can cost up to £22, so it's not cheap. But what with my allotment in Hastings and all the spaces I've planted trees in, it's all good fun.'

There were some logistics, it turned out. Clive was meticulous about planning his campaigns.

'I used to have a map which I would colour in, with every space which had trees, every space which could do with a tree and every space where I planted one. But it just got to be too much to maintain after a while. But I still know pretty much where everything is. It does get to be like a bit of a military campaign. I got a copy of *The Art of War* by Sun Tzu. It's got so much in there, it's all so true even now.'

Perhaps Clive was thinking of the Sun Tzu saying: '*The best thing of all is to take the enemy's country whole and intact; to shatter and destroy it is not so good.*'

Any campaign has setbacks, I suggested. Clive furrowed his brow and his smile disappeared for a moment.

'It can be annoying when a tree you've planted gets removed. Sometimes it's because a house changes hands, and the new owners don't even know what it is they're getting rid of. That kills me, it's so stupid.'

He clenched his fists. Was he ever tempted to deal out vengeance on the unbelievers?

'I did once think about planting some Japanese knotweed by a local building, but I didn't in the end. It would only have been a nuisance and that's not what I'm about.'

So what were his ambitions for the future?

'I want to keep planting trees and getting other people to plant. We could all plant a fruit tree or a native tree. It all makes a difference, doesn't it?'

We smiled, shook our hands and took our leave of Clive. As we walked through the park, we wondered which plants were planned and which Clive and his fellow guerrillas had introduced. On the face of it, guerrilla gardening seemed a benign form of anarchy. What would the world look like if everyone planted one tree, somewhere? We might find out, one day. For now, it was time to plan a train trip…

TOMSK

For years I have travelled on London Underground's Metropolitan line. Near the terminus at Amersham, there's a little branch line, a detour to Chesham where I used to work. Once, many years ago, the Chesham branch line was busy, in all likelihood. Now it's no more than an afterthought. From time to time, rumours spring up of its impending closure, but it has yet to happen. My theory is that the Chesham line survives by keeping ever so quiet, until the rumours go away.

I thought of Chesham when looking at the map and planning my trip to Tomsk. For the Metropolitan line, read the Trans-Siberian Railway; for Chesham, read Tomsk. Just like Chesham, it's on a little branch line away from the main route. It is possible, and normal, to travel from Moscow to Tomsk by air in four hours. The same journey by train is a Siberian mammoth 56 hours long. I had never attempted any of the world's great railway journeys and this seemed to be the opportunity to do so – as long as I didn't fall asleep at the wrong moment, and wake up in Vladivostock.

The internet directed me to one of those helpful websites that takes the pain out of your decision making. I forget its name. There are so many of them now. There are so many that the web can now eat itself, by creating websites that compare websites for you, such as price comparison websites. If I have the time, I might take the next step in the evolution of the internet, and create a price comparison website comparison website.

Anyway, while this website was helpful, I felt the need to talk to another human soul. A few minutes later, Alexei was on the line. He may be wondering, even now, why the caller seemed on the verge of hysterical laughter throughout the conversation.

When a new market is saturated, one way to make your product stand out is distinctive advertising. This was achieved by the TV advertising of one of those price comparison websites. Imagine someone's study. He is well-read (plenty of books), well-dressed (a stylish silk dressing gown), confident and persuasive. He is called Aleksandr. He is also a meerkat.

The advertisements allow Aleksandr to rail against a fictitious stupid human audience who, he says, cannot tell the difference between comparethemarket.com and his own website, comparethemeerkat.com. He uses two flipcharts, and recordings of jingles for the two websites, to point out the difference.

I've worked with advertising executives many times. Five-eighths of Buckinghamshire would now be mine, if any of those executives had promoted my employers' services with ideas half as clever as comparethemeerkat.com. Whether Aleksandr was born from hours of perusing the M section of dictionaries, or afternoons inhaling Arbroath smoky concentrate, is a mystery.

I must have had something useful to do, instead of which I went online to see if comparethemeerkat.com is a real website. It is. Someone with too much time on their hands has spared no effort to ensure that, if you want to see a large meerkat from Agra whose main hobby is darts, you can. If you then want to compare the said meerkat with a medium sized specimen from Cairo who is a ballerina, you can do that, too.

And then there's the extra touch of genius, the cherry on the top. Some twisted imagination decided that it wasn't enough to create a meerkat in a silk dressing gown. He had to be a meerkat in a silk dressing gown with a Russian accent. Aleksandr now has more friends on Facebook than Vladimir Putin and Roman Abramovich put together, and quite right, too.

So, when Alexei from the nameless website came on the line, and started speaking in that distinctive Russian accent which sounds as if there is a pound of treacle in the speaker's throat, I found the conversation difficult. It is bound to be hard to talk to someone when you're fighting the temptation to ask them to compare meerkats for you. I struggled on regardless.

'Tomsk is long journey from Moscow,' said Alexei. This seemed to come from the Douglas Adams school of self-evident geography: space is big, really big, etc. I asked about timetables. There was a long pause.

'Only odd days,' said Alexei.

What did he mean, odd days? Had someone ripped pages out of his timetable?

'Tomsk train only runs on odd days. Not even days. Third, fifth, seventh and so on. Also there is only one train a day.'

This was going to be a challenge.

* * *

Time travels at different speeds in different parts of the universe, according to Einstein. Now the trouble with Einstein, to paraphrase Ken Dodd, is that he never played the Glasgow Empire on a Saturday night after Rangers and Celtic had both lost. Einstein is right, though, about time. It travels at different speeds in different parts of the Trans-Siberian Express, never mind anywhere else.

You find this out when you forsake the simple comfort of your four-bed compartment, for a general wander along the train or – for Helen and me – for an expedition to the dining car. You take care not to trip up on the thin green carpet with the flowery pattern that snakes along the corridor. You edge past the timetable on the wall that lists every stop, the arrival times and the period of time that the train will halt at each station. Just beyond the timetable, you employ a crab technique to get past someone else: a teenage boy in T-shirt and shorts, playing a handheld computer game, or an older man plugging his razor into an adaptor socket, or a mother getting respite from her family by gazing out of the window at the birches and the purple lupins and the giant hogweed.

The gentle sway of the carriage tips you towards the half-open doors of other compartments. In traditional British manner, you pretend not to notice the occupants, eating Pot Noodles or reading novels or brushing their children's hair. It is all very relaxed and informal; a far cry from the type of hotel in which we stayed in Moscow, the night before getting the train. (Guests staying in the posh rooms on the 6th-16th floors used different lifts in a different reception lobby from the riff-raff; we were on the 27th floor.)

By now, you're almost at the end of the carriage. You pause to look at the *samovar*, the heavy metal container that Russians use to heat water, and to admire the dials and readings that tell you the water temperature and how much water is inside. If *samovars* ever run dry, there'll be another Russian Revolution. The carriage sways again as you pass the small room where a *provodnitsa* (carriage attendant) sits, listening to the radio or playing cards or chatting with one of her colleagues. *Provodnitsas* are the blonde, blue-uniformed antibodies of the train. As it winds its way like a multicoloured millipede through the landscape, they keep its insides tidy and ensure that it ingests and expels the right diet of passengers at the right times.

Bungo has a drink on the Trans-Siberian...

You stumble past the toilet, and the electronic display above your head telling you whether it is occupied or free, along with time, date and temperature information. Then you pull open the door at the end of the carriage and step into a no-man's-land of darkness between your carriage and the next. You are no longer insulated from the sounds of the train, or the smell of fumes. The floor bucks and writhes beneath your feet like a reluctant rodeo horse. A spaghetti of yellow wires hangs from the ceiling, tangling with your hair. Everything is faster, heavier, noisier, smellier, more dangerous. You clutch your keys to ensure they don't drop down the gap between the carriages and out into Siberia.

You reach for the far door and push it open. Sometimes it bangs into the back of a *provodnitsa* who is washing the floor, but usually you can go through, unobstructed, into the mini-community of the next carriage, and resume your odyssey as the noise and the smell and the movement die down once more. Everything is back to a more sedate pace.

As the train munched up the miles, we went in search of lunch. Not only does time run at different rates in the carriages and the in-between spaces; the dining car is in a different time zone from the rest of the train. The train as a whole runs on Moscow time, but the dining car runs on 'local time' – which, at some point of the journey, is two hours ahead of Moscow, which in turn becomes three hours ahead of Moscow by the time it reaches Tomsk. It is easy to make the mistake of leaving your watch on Moscow time and turning up very late indeed for your meal.

Each carriage has its own colours. The approach to the dining car was an unprepossessing battleship grey.

'Mmm,' I said as a smell wafted towards me. 'Something good's cooking.'

As we reached the restaurant, we found the source of the smell: various items of clothing hung on the walls to dry. The laundry made an unusual counterpoint to the plush red tablecloths and the small net curtains, with their graphics of a train and tree and the legend TOMICH (Tomsk in Cyrillic). We persuaded a bored-looking young member of staff to interrupt her card game and hand us a menu.

'The dining car gives complex dinners,' it said. After some consideration, we chose soup starters: *borscht* for Helen, a hot and spicy *solyanka* for me.

'Have you noticed something?' asked Helen, as I was halfway through a spoonful.

I thought she meant the topping of sour cream and dill which was common to both soups (and much other food we would eat, on the train and in Tomsk). But that wasn't it. The dining car had gone silent and still. The train had stopped: not at a station, but in the middle of nowhere. We had become used to the rhythm of the train, even in the few hours we had been on board; it had slowed so gently that we had barely noticed.

As we finished our soup and handed the plates to the staff, the train began to move once again.

'Do you think they waited till we'd finished the soup?'

'Well, it is quite hard to eat soup on a train...'

We giggled our way through a second course. I chose 'bourgeois surprise', and it was, as the menu had promised, complex: the pineapple slice I was expecting on top of the beef turned out to be an orange segment. Then we made our way back, losing two hours in the corridors as we returned from 'local time' to Moscow time, to catch up with the other occupants of our compartment in carriage 11.

Although Helen and I were only on the train for 56 hours, five other people occupied the two bunk beds opposite us during that time. They were all Russians taking workaday journeys rather than holidays, as far as we could tell. We were, it seemed, the only non-Russians on the train during the whole journey – unless you count Bungo, accompanying us for this trip as an unobtrusive inhabitant of my hand luggage.

First to join us in our compartment, as the train left Moscow, was a woman of generous dimensions, in her fifties with henna red hair, squareish spectacles and a dress with large rose motifs, supplemented by a top and leggings. A delicate gold watch was conspicuous on her left wrist. She showed us a photo of her son, who was in the army. Joining the train at the same time, and residing on the lower opposite bunk bed, was a younger woman, in her twenties, also with reddish hair and what tennis commentators call puppy fat, wearing a yellow dress. She was an avid reader of Boris Akunin detective stories.

Neither our Russian – well, Helen's Russian, as I don't speak the language – nor the ladies' English were clear enough to the other parties to lead to any great conversations. However, as I lay on the top bunk that night struggling to get to sleep, it was obvious that the younger woman was fluent in the international language of snoring.

By Kirov station the following morning, both ladies had gone. We had one co-habitee for the next 24 hours: Yuri, a tall man in early middle age with close-cropped greying hair and a T-shirt with a pattern of thin purple and green hoops. Yuri was returning to his wife and four children in Tyumen.

Yuri had bought a stuffed hedgehog toy from one of the many women selling their wares on the platform at Kirov. As we live near an animal hospital that specialises in treating injured hedgehogs, Helen struck up a conversation with Yuri on this theme, drawing hedgehog pictures on her notepad to help things along. Miles Kington used to use 'Franglais' – an amalgam of English and French – and now Helen was pioneering the new mixed dialect of Rusglish.

We were a puzzle to Yuri. For some reason, he thought we came from Liverpool, though this may have been influenced by his knowledge of English Premier League football teams. Manchester United, Chelsea (and their Russian owner), Liverpool and Everton were all familiar to him, but Arsenal and Tottenham were not. Liverpool had not won the English Premier League – or First Division, as it was – for 20 years, so perhaps Yuri's knowledge was of the nostalgic variety.

Like many other people we have met on our foreign travels, he had heard of Margaret Thatcher ('good'); like some of those people, he had also heard of Tony Blair ('not so good'). The recent formation of a UK coalition government did not register in Yuri's awareness of foreign politics.

The biggest puzzle to Yuri was why we wanted to visit Tomsk.

'Not Lake Baikal?' he asked.

We shook our heads. In fairness to Yuri, we had received the same reaction from UK travel agents when we were planning the trip. And it's hard to explain to a Russian why Elisabeth Beresford didn't name one of her characters after Novosibirsk, or Irkutsk.

Nonetheless, we liked Yuri and he liked us enough to buy us ice creams at one of the station stops. For himself, he obtained a shrink-wrapped portion of chicken and potatoes for dinner... but nothing with which to eat it. Yuri was a patient man – anybody who eats chicken with a teaspoon has to be. Perhaps he was better at organising others than himself, as he helped us to get glasses in splendid metal cupholders from which we could drink our supplies of fruit tea.

Yuri was a sound sleeper. He might have missed his stop at Tyumen the next morning, if a middle-aged *provodnitsa* had not come into the compartment to wake him with a friendly pat on the bottom.

As Yuri wandered off along the platform of Tyumen's smart new station, we awaited our next companions. My initial reservations about sharing with strangers had lessened and mutated into curiosity; this was a real-life cabaret. Would the next people be a couple? Old? Young? On the run? If they snored too loudly or misbehaved, would I be able to raise an Alan Sugar finger and say: 'You're fired'?

Confounding all my guesses, a young woman in a white T-shirt, black trousers and shoes with a hint of bling entered the compartment. Accompanying her was a little girl of about three years of age with floppy blonde hair, a white sweatshirt top, turquoise trousers and blue socks. In her left hand, the little girl carried a white teddy bear with a red nose, red soles on its feet and a black bowler hat on its head.

Mother and daughter were going to Tomsk, so they would be our final companions. They knew less English than Yuri, but we exchanged smiles – especially when it became clear that we had something they wanted. The mother had brought an impressive set of props to keep her daughter occupied: a book of stories to read to her, a square board into which the little girl could insert pegs of different colours and a clutch of colouring pens. The trouble was that she didn't have enough paper on which to draw. Helen provided some from her notepad – problem solved, happy infant.

Our final afternoon and evening passed in peace: listening to the announcements at each station (always from female voices); eating a bag of strawberries we bought on the platform at Omsk and lifting our feet off the floor in unison as a *provodnitsa* vacuumed the compartment. The strawberries, by the way, cost the equivalent of £2.25 for two and a quarter pounds in weight. Never mind the euro or the dollar: our national currency had achieved parity with a fruit.

The only stain on the day came as evening fell. I reached for my cup of cranberry and raspberry tea – too late. The little girl, roaming round the floor, raised her hand to the table on which the cup rested, knocking it to the floor. Somehow the hot tea avoided the girl, her mother, Helen and me, adding an interesting new pattern to the carpet. A little mopping up by everyone, and we upheld the finest British traditions of keeping calm and carrying on.

Before we knew it, morning had come and the train was drawing into Tomsk. The girl's attention had been focused on her toys until now, but her mother had packed everything away. I reached into my overnight bag, pulled out Bungo and introduced him to the little girl. She was happy enough to cuddle him until the train stopped. I retrieved Bungo from her arms, gave her and her mother a final wave, avoided the tea stains on the carpet and followed Helen out onto the platform.

***

That cup of tea seemed like a drop in the ocean as we watched the teenage boys half-walking, half-running in our direction.

'Oh, my God!' exclaimed Natasha. 'I'm so sorry, I forgot to mention… this happens every year on this day.'

We were standing above the banks of the river Tom, on our way round Tomsk with Natasha as our guide.

'Every year, on this day, people run around Tomsk with buckets of water and pour them over people,' Natasha continued.

The boys advanced, brandishing their buckets in meaningful ways. We'd already been drenched by a shower on our first day in Tomsk, which had broken Helen's umbrella. In a measured, in-no-way-am-I-panicking manner, she slid her camera beneath her jacket. I thought about asking after the origins of this unsociable Tomsk ritual, but decided not to. We kept walking. This was not life-threatening – unless we got pneumonia, maybe – but nor was it the type of welcome I'd been expecting.

My attention had been so fixed on the bucket-wielders that I hadn't noticed anyone else around, until the boys came to a sudden halt. Sitting on a bench, between us and them, were two old ladies. One of them fixed the teenage terrors with a firm stare and said a few words. This odd tableau lasted a few seconds, and then the boys crossed to the other side of the road, not looking back. I hadn't seen old ladies help other people across the road before; their intervention was well timed.

Natasha, Helen and I had now reached Tomsk's most famous monument: a 'sarcastic landmark', as Natasha put it. This was a statue of Anton Chekhov who, among other things, coined the theatrical maxim known as Chekhov's

Gun: 'If in Act I you have a pistol hanging on the wall, then it must fire in the last act.' He might have been gratified to know that you can apply this theory to buckets of water, too. We saw the bucket-wielding teenagers later in the day, soaking fellow teenagers up and down Lenin Prospekt.

The statue of Chekhov may be unique, as a town's collective response to criticism. The writer visited Tomsk on his way to the far east of Siberia – an arduous journey, through land still recovering from the previous winter, involving river steamers, horse-drawn carriages and trains.

Chekhov did not arrive at Tomsk in the best of moods. He wrote to his sister: 'I have nothing for dinner. Sensible people usually take twenty pounds of provisions when they go to Tomsk. It seems I was a fool and so I have fed for a fortnight on nothing but milk and eggs...'

The journey was already causing his shoulders and collarbone to ache (and, as a doctor, Chekhov would have been painfully able to diagnose himself), with the occasional extra fun of head pains, chest pains and haemorrhoids.

Flooding caused many of the roads in and around Tomsk to become almost impassable, but Chekhov got there in mid-May 1890: 'All the Tomsk people tell me that there has not been a spring so cold and rainy as this one since 1842. Half Tomsk is under water. My luck!'

Chekhov's verdict on Tomsk was not complimentary: 'Tomsk is a very dull town. To judge from the drunkards whose acquaintance I have made, and from the intellectual people who have come to the hotel to pay their respects to me, the inhabitants are very dull too.' He told his publisher AS Suvorin that 'Tomsk is a dull and intemperate town. There are absolutely no good-looking women, and the disregard for justice is Asiatic. The town is remarkable for the fact that governors die in it.' Even distance did not lend enchantment to his view – his next stop Krasnoyarsk was 'a picturesque, cultured town; compared with it, Tomsk is "a pig in a skullcap"'.

He picked on the wrong pig; this one bit back. The statue in Tomsk depicts Chekhov in floppy hat and long coat, hands behind his back cradling an umbrella, his bearded face drooping in disapproval. His feet, splayed in classic Chaplin fashion at ten to two, are bare.

'This is because his shoes have been stolen,' explained Natasha. 'This shows Chekhov as he might have been viewed by one of those drunkards he complained about. Chekhov was not nice about Tomsk. He only liked one thing and that was a restaurant. He did not like our men, our women, our markets. So – Chekhov is unpleasant about Tomsk – Tomsk is unpleasant about Chekhov.'

I could understand why Natasha was so unequivocal about it. If someone called you a pig in a skullcap, you wouldn't like it, either. And it could have been worse for the real Chekhov; someone might have dumped a bucket of water over him.

***

It's not as if Russians are unused to criticism of their country. We British have been giving them stick for centuries, right back to 1553 when a small fleet of merchant ships led by Richard Chancellor landed at Archangel. The crew met Ivan the Terrible, who granted trade privileges to Britain.

From that point, a succession of merchants, diplomats, doctors, engineers and traders came, saw and used reports, journals, books and letters to disparage: a sort of *veni, vidi, bitchi.*

Chancellor himself got in a few early jibes at the Russians' religious practices, damning them as 'such excess of superstition, as the like hath not been heard of'. George Turberville, secretary to a diplomatic mission in 1568, described his hosts as 'bloody, rude and blind'. One of the Russians' main vices, this British political and professional elite told its readers, was drunkenness. 'To drink drunke, is an ordinary matter with them every day in the weeke', wrote Giles Fletcher, a late 16th century ambassador in Moscow. Almost a century later, Dr Samuel Collins described carnival 'debauchery and luxury... they drink as if they were never to drink more'. John Perry, who served as a naval engineer with Peter the Great, condemned the drinking of priests and congregations on Church festivals. Russians gained a reputation for dishonesty, corruption and deviousness. Anthony Jenkinson, captain of the *Primrose*, which sailed to Russia in 1557, wrote that 'They are great talkers and liars, flatterers and dissemblers', while Perry only received salary for one of the fourteen years in which he worked in Russia.

To add to their unflattering profile, the Russian treatment of women came in for strong criticism. Turberville wrote that they kept their wives in 'a cruel and almost Asiatic seclusion' and Collins noted that 'If a man kill his slave, or his wife, in correcting them, there is no law against them', while 'A woman that kills her husband is buried alive'. Few of these early British visitors acknowledged the existence of any worthwhile Russian culture. Collins described Russians as 'wholly devoted to their own Ignorance'.

By the late 18th century, tutors such as William Coxe were chaperoning young British aristocrats through Russia and Scandinavia, and the reforms of the 'Greats', Peter and Catherine, had evoked some Western admiration. Even so, Coxe wrote of 'many instances of the grossest barbarism [which] fell under our observation' and of 'indolence, which appears almost national'. Coxe did praise the Russians' hospitality, and judged that the reforms of Peter and Catherine had helped Russia in 'proceeding towards civilization [but] they are still far removed from that state'. By the late Victorian era, British visitors to Russia took a more positive view of their hosts: as the evidence of Russian cultural sophistication, political and military power was undeniable, and Britain's ruling of the waves was beginning to be challenged as never before.

But, compared with centuries of British criticism of Russians as drunk, lazy, superstitious, corrupt, misogynistic liars with no culture of their own, I reckoned Chekhov hadn't been too unkind about his fellow countrymen. It's lucky that all those British visitors didn't come to Tomsk. We wouldn't have been able to move for statues.

***

As it is, Tomskians have more than just Chekhov to admire in statue form. Near our hotel, at the northern end of the city, stood the figure of another man. Like Chekhov, he was protected from cold and rain by a long coat but, unlike Chekhov, he had no umbrella. His feet were properly shod. One hand stretched out, arm almost parallel to the ground, inviting the people to follow him in creating a new type of society. Here, on a traffic island in a street bearing his name, was Lenin.

Behind him was the peach-coloured Epiphany Cathedral; to his left, on another traffic island, a small pink building with a blue roof decorated with stars, the tiny Iverskaya Chapel. But, as you might expect, Lenin ignored them both. Nor did he pay any heed to the eight men tending the flowerbeds beneath him on his island. He pointed down Lenin Prospekt, to a glorious future – or, if you prefer, to the concrete brutalism of the town's main theatre. Almost 90 years after his death, Lenin was still pointing, posing and looking bossy: a typical Bungo.

But nobody was listening to Lenin now. To people of Natasha's age, he was part of the distant past. Natasha was 21, a recent graduate from Tomsk's Polytechnic University in Translation and Linguistics and married to a regional manager who oversees telecommunications installations in the wider region outside Tomsk. She hoped to work as an interpreter.

'I want to stay in Tomsk,' she said. 'I was born here, I studied at university here. My family and friends are here. I was in the Czech Republic for half a year as an exchange student... but I missed my family too much. I could never leave here.

'My husband says that every village is the same round here... the theatre is on the right... the cultural centre is on the left... all planned by the Soviets to look exactly the same.'

Lenin once said that Communism was Soviet power plus the electrification of the whole country. For Natasha, perhaps, post-Communist Russia was market economics plus better telecommunications.

'After the Soviet Union fell, one of Russia's most successful businessmen introduced a national game for students,' she remembered. 'It involved us having to think about economics, politics, everything. I enjoyed it very much. Now Russia is joining the political system.'

The system which Lenin and revolution brought to the Soviet Union – which Natasha is too young to remember – is not forgotten in Tomsk. In a side street off Lenin Prospekt, out of the bright afternoon sunlight and down stone steps, lies the Museum of Oppression, in the old offices of the NKVD, the forerunners of the KGB. This is Tomsk's 'sarcastic' (to use Natasha's favourite English word) tribute to life in the USSR.

The star of the show – surprise, surprise – is Lenin. He has his own room commemorating him in an impressive array of physical forms. You can admire Lenin as tapestry, Lenin on medals, Lenin in wood and in money, Lenin in mosaic and on banners. There is a collection of over 50 badges made in 1967 to commemorate the 50th anniversary of the Revolution. Various busts and small statues depict him, always clasping his left lapel with his hand. Postcards printed in 1980 mark the 110th anniversary of his birth; stamps from the previous year celebrate the 109th anniversary.

Now, if someone – my grandmother, for example – had lived to the age of 109, I would celebrate her birthday as a magnificent feat of endurance. Where is the achievement in being born 109 years ago – and being dead? It seems a little desperate. Maybe postcard and stamp sales were providing that extra income which Brezhnev and his Politburo needed to keep the Soviets in the arms race. If that was the case, it only proves the truth of the old saying: philately will get you nowhere.

The next room expounds at length on the wartime work of the NKVD. Then another room – numbered 59 for no obvious reason – is an empty cell, except for the wooden benches on which prisoners would sit. Next door is a reproduction of a commandant's office: the desk, the files, the phone and the anglepoise lamp. I sat in the chair opposite the standing waxwork of the commandant and tried not to confess anything.

The final room in the museum relates more to the 1930s, by which time Lenin was long dead and Stalin was the USSR's leader, father, confessor and more. But his presence in this room is more shadowy, restricted to one or two wall photographs. In the middle of the room is a montage, in the shape of a cross, showing the faces of Tomsk people whom the NKVD caught, and executed in the 1930s. The display notes their dates of capture and dates of execution. The figure 23,000, on a piece of paper, flutters at the centre of the cross. We walked out of the room, up the stairs and into the sunlight, thinking of all those who never did.

***

Tomsk's origins go back to 1604, when Boris Godunov sent 200 Cossacks to establish a fortress, and a local tribal leader ceded the land. In its time, it has been a regional centre of government, a magnet for gold prospectors, a home for political exiles and a centre of White Army resistance after the Revolution. But right now, this old city has a young face. Its heart is Troitsky Skver Park – or New Cathedral Park as Natasha called it; there was a cathedral here, but the Soviets knocked it down.

It would be stretching a point to call the park peaceful on the day we visited: the fountains proved irresistible for those bucket-wielders. Those doing the drenching were boys; most of those being drenched, and shrieking and giggling with shock and pleasure, were girls. Small children and adults escaped the treatment. A 'ponies for hire' service did brisk business; other children trundled along the paths, steering miniature 4 x 4 vehicles as if they had never concentrated on anything so much in their lives. One little boy in a blue top zoomed past in a toy Ducati, complete with tiny stabilisers.

The only impediment to our enjoyment of this scene was the drift of small white particles through the summer sky. At first glance they appeared to be thistledown; we found out later that they came from poplar trees. They had the irritating knack of flying straight for our eyes or nostrils. But at least the poplar snow didn't appear at the same time as the local midges, whose bites left their marks for weeks afterwards.

Helen and I found a park bench and, dodging the poplar snow, got to grips with our *blinis*. Russian cuisine doesn't have a great reputation – even chicken Kiev may have been the invention of a Frenchman – but *blinis* are one of its pleasures. They are Russia's version of fast food; fluffy yeast-based pancakes which you can eat as they are, or with a bewildering array of fillings. On a previous visit to Moscow, our cavernous hotel had concealed a *blini* bar in which we'd had a three course meal of *blini* starter, main and dessert. *Blini* outlets were dotted around Tomsk, including one in New Cathedral Park. I opted for a meat filling and Helen chose cheese. *Blinis* have three things in their favour. They're easy to make; they're filling and tasty;

and they're cheap. And, in a city with as many students as Tomsk, sources of cheap, easy fast food are crucial.

'Tomsk has 500,000 inhabitants and also 100,000 students,' Natasha told us. 'That's why it is called the Siberian Athens.'

Behind us in the park was a statue of St Tatiana, the patron saint of students. She gets her name from the mother of the first Russian education minister, who established Russia's first university in 1755. Her saint day on 25 September is a public holiday as well as a 'students' day'. This sounded to me like a good wheeze to get students a day off.

Tomsk has six universities – so the city has rather more brainpower than its Womble namesake. Natasha showed us around the two best known. Tomsk State University dates back to 1878 when it was the first university in Siberia, and the first to admit women. As Helen and I are alumni of the first British university to admit women, we felt a natural affinity here – though the similarities did not extend to Tomsk's version having a stuffed man on public display in its cloisters.

In its early years, Tomsk's academic staff included Ivan Pavlov, whose famous research into conditional reflexes involved recording the reactions of dogs when food arrived. He would signal the arrival of food not only with a bell – as the myth has it – but with other methods such as metronomes, tuning forks and even electric shocks. The dogs may have decided, in due course, that Tomsk was not where they wanted to be; we saw a mere handful during our time in the city.

Natasha's heart was with TSU's near-neighbour, Tomsk Polytechnic University, where she studied. Her step had a new spring to it as we passed through the entrance and up a smart marble staircase. This is the oldest technical university in Siberia, but it has kept up with academic and management trends including, it seems, management-speak. At the top of the staircase, a large notice told us the University's mission:

'... *to advance knowledge and experience, allowing any individual, society, and Russia as a whole to assess and introduce the best methods of training for the highly qualified specialists and to bring about innovations in the sphere of science and university education...*'

I was more out of breath from reading the mission statement than from climbing the stairs.

'We now have National Research status,' said Natasha with obvious pride. 'This means we should attract more students. Our courses are better than the State University because everyone learns languages, along with their chosen academic subject.'

So how much did it cost to study at this tower of academic excellence?

'It is free if you pass the entrance exam.' Natasha paused. 'Or if you are related to the Rector.'

For all her sensible appearance – short and slim, fair hair in a neat ponytail, black top and trousers, black shoes – and deadpan delivery, Natasha had a sense of humour. On Shishkova Street, she showed us the Shushkin House, an example of the old wooden houses that are still around in Tomsk, but rare now in the rest of Siberia. The house gets its name from a Russian writer who was exiled to Tomsk. Exile was more comfortable for him than for some: he had one house in which to live and another, next door, in which to write. I asked about the decorations near the roof.

'They show how superstitious Russians are,' Natasha replied with a smile. 'They are to keep bad spirits from flying into the house.'

We loved the intricacy of the decorations around the windows, and later visited several more in Krasnoarmeyskaya Street: the Russo-German house (now used to promote cultural relations between Russia

Old wooden house, Tomsk

and Germany, though it started this work in 1939, a fine example of bad timing if ever there was one), the Peacock House and the Dragon House.

Natasha had one last sight to show us. We hopped on the bus and headed to the southern end of Lenin Prospekt, and Lagerny Gardens. Two stones flank the entrance: one has '1941' carved into it, the other '1945'. Avenues of birch and lime trees flank a central stretch of flowerbed. At the far end, steps lead up to an eternal flame and the largest of Tomsk's many statues: a mother handing a gun to her son, to enable him to defend Mother Russia. Beyond the statue is a view of the river Tom. Either side of the statue and steps, lines of memorial stones list the names of Tomskians who fought and died in World War II. The only dates are birthdates – 'probably because nobody could be sure when some of them died,' according to Natasha. Whatever the reason, the effect is poignant: from the birthdate, you can calculate how old these men would be now.

'My grandfather fought,' was Natasha's simple comment. 'He met my grandmother afterwards. They were both married to other people before the war.'

She shook our hands: this was the end of our guided tour. We watched as she walked back towards the main street. If Natasha represented the future for Tomsk and Russia, then the future was in good hands.

A minute or two later, as we stood in front of the statue, a burst of singing came from nowhere: no, not from nowhere – from a number of freestanding speakers among the trees. It seemed that this music played every daylight hour, on the hour, *a cappella* remembrance.

We started our slow walk back towards the city centre.

The sky began to weep, a few drops at first, then bucketing down. A fierce wind got up, twisting Helen's umbrella inside out until it was beyond repair.

***

Was Robert Burns right? If we could see ourselves as others see us, would it free us from blunders and foolish notions? The football-loving Trans-Siberian fellow traveller, Yuri, had given us some glimpse of his view of the British. Now, a few minutes up the road from our hotel in Tomsk, sat the terrible temptation of the self-styled 'Stonebridge English Pub'.

I confess to a degree of hypocrisy at this point. I've tried to avoid ersatz English or British or Irish tourist attractions outside the British Isles. The Irish pub in Bratislava survived without my custom. I came close to committing murder on my honeymoon in Florence, when a short, bald and over-excited Scotsman rushed up to me in the middle of the Uffizi Gallery to declaim: 'I've found a pub where they serve Guinness!'

Yet I've enjoyed the easy laughs available from bars and restaurants in various foreign climes. On a previous visit to Russia, a St Petersburg restaurant had themed its menu options according to the class struggle. The 'Tsar's banquet' options (sturgeon Suarov-style, quail's eggs) competed for our roubles with 'proletariat' choices including 'true Russian lard' and 'lovely chicken giblets'. I had *solyanka* and duck, which must have made me middle-class: no surprise there. On this trip, I'd seen a leaflet for a Moscow restaurant specialising in traditional Russian 'home-made style cooking', such as 'Don style ear pie' and 'goose foot in a pot'. Now it was time to put the boot on the other (goose) foot. We wandered down the stairs to the Tomsk hotel basement, which had an English pub.

They'd got some of the details right, for sure. It was dark, brown and wooden. Stools were placed at careful intervals to cause maximum obstruction. A large TV screen played pop videos and football to nobody. The wall decorations showed that the pub owner's research had gone beyond the normal London clichés: no Tower Bridge, beefeaters, Houses of Parliament or London Eye.

On the other hand, the world knows that an Englishman's home is his castle; if you looked round this pub, you might conclude that we live in little else. 18th century engravings depicted the castles of Dudley and Linlithgow, Arundel and Denbigh, though Lewes Priory and St John's Gate in 'Clerkenwell, Middlesex' were also there on the walls. As a giggling blonde teenager gave us menus, my eye searched for those items which symbolise the best of British cuisine: fish and chips; the roast beef of old(e) England(e); apple pie. They weren't there. The chef might have overdosed on 'Sherwood Forest's mushroom refreshments' before compiling his or her version of an English menu. You could enjoy a drink with a choice of snacks, 'dried horse beef' or 'dried smelt bellies'. Meat lovers could indulge themselves further in the strange land of 'Meat-shire', including cold meats that were 'James Cook's favourite'. The 'Cheese Kingdom' implied that the British Empire was larger than anyone had thought, with its 'Kamamber' and Parmesan.

If you wanted to get wider still and wider, a hot appetizer of London Classical Stew or British Kingdom Fisherman Soup would be just the thing. The salads had their own distinctive (non-vegetarian) take. London Salad comprised turkey fillet with a 'provansal' sauce, while York Salad – boiled beef and carrots – was the closest item on the menu to a traditional British dish.

I went for English Channel Salad, with its groundbreaking combination of eel, radish, cabbage and chips producing a curious result of forgettable blandness. As we were only stopping for a light lunch, this precluded trying the 'pickles from an Essex village', which was a shame.

So there it was, one Russian view of the British through their pubs and food: old, dark brown, wooden and bland. Thank goodness Chekhov didn't visit any English pubs.

***

The owl and the pussycat went to sea in a beautiful pea green boat. If they'd been travelling by plane, they might have chosen Siberian Airlines. Thanks to modern low-cost airlines, we are used to seeing planes as giant mobile advertising boards; Siberian Airlines takes this further, marinating the length of its planes in owl and pussycat pea green. Does that make them Lear jets?

As Helen and I sat on our flight from Tomsk to Moscow and wrestled with the choice of in-flight meal – 'chicken or meat' – I looked out of the window, down at the huge landmass we were leaving. I could see why Yuri and the travel agents had been puzzled about our choice of destination. Tomsk is a working town, not a tourist trap, with a down-to-earth attitude: as different as you could imagine from the elegant melancholy of St Petersburg, or the brashness of Moscow, awash with bling ancient (the Kremlin), past (the Metro marble and chandeliers) and present (theme parks, stretch limousines and global brands wherever you looked). Nonetheless, Tomsk's future may be bright, as it uses its wealth from the surrounding oil fields and trains all those students to run the Russia of the future. Tomsk the town is a lot cleverer than Tomsk the Womble.

Siberia is not a region with world renown as a holiday hotspot, but we had enjoyed our time in Tomsk. The town's pavements and flowerbeds were of almost Womble-like levels of tidiness. It was a surprise to find frozen mushrooms available, loose, in the supermarkets (picking wild mushrooms is a Russian, and Womble-esque, obsession).

We would have been happy to spend more time eating *blinis* in the park and elaborate evening meals in our hotel's Italian restaurant, where the portly, bearded, middle-aged pianist with a weary air reminded me of the late John Ogdon. Now, though, it was time to come home, and plan the next stage of my quest…

CHOLET

'Let's split up,' I whispered. 'He can't track both of us.'

The man had been following us ever since we'd gone inside. He was a good choice for surveillance: a young-old face on which you couldn't nail down the precise age, or find any expression; white hair that was neither curly nor straight. He'd done this many times before. That much was obvious from the way he stopped, every so often, as we stopped, without meeting our eyes or avoiding them.

Just two things let him down. The top surveillance men don't wear bright white sweaters. Someone had washed it that morning, judging by its pristine state. White's all right if you're a real ghost, not one of MI5's or the KGB's. It's hard to be inconspicuous in white. The other problem was the walk. Only one word can describe it: a mince. If it's hard to pass unnoticed wearing white, it's even harder to act menacing when you mince. I've spent years working with musical theatre people – trust me on this.

There were no crowds of people between him and us. We had passed a couple of bored, skinny teenagers smoking in the doorway, but they wouldn't be any help. I was getting trigger-happy. It was time to give Monsieur Hopkirk something new to think about.

In perfect concert, Helen went to the left and I went to the right. There was no obvious cover, so I ducked into a confessional. The space was so black that my head met the brickwork. For a moment, the air in Sacre Coeur threatened to turn sacre bleu. After a moment, I steadied myself and focused on the target. *Forgive me, Father, for I am about to sin.*

It was essential to keep still. I took final aim, and pressed the button. Into the silence and darkness of the confessional, the click and whirr and flash of my camera dropped like the largest, most metallic pin ever. But my aim was true and, with the help of a camera, I had achieved my objective. I peered out of the darkness at the bizarre beauty in front of me.

Two banks of four tall, thin windows, on either side of six taller windows, blasted my eyes with a symphony of pink and gold art deco stained glass. Below them, picked out in yellow, was the shape of a bat. The thought of whether Gotham City's finest was a churchgoer had not crossed my mind before. Did the priest send a searchlight up into the night sky to indicate forthcoming services?

'To the Bat Church, Robin!'

If Sacre Coeur in Cholet was the Caped Crusader's church of choice, he had unusual but excellent taste. The redbrick interior and the blaze of light from the stained glass windows combined in a Roman-Byzantine splendour which made me wonder how long the church had been here. In fact, it had been built during the Second World War. Not that it was overflowing with worshippers on this wet Saturday afternoon. Menacing, mincing Monsieur Hopkirk was the only other person there, apart from a middle-aged lady rearranging the flowers on the altar, oblivious to everything behind her.

Helen and I had sat on the wooden chairs for a while, in contemplation. We had been about to take some photos when he turned up. His beady stare had fixed on us, as if in silent admonition - hence the game of *grandmere's* footsteps which had led us both around the church, trying to take photos without him noticing.

Church in Cholet

There weren't enough pillars for us to hide behind, but our retreat to the confessionals on each side seemed to confuse him. We took a few pictures, paused for a few moments as we admired the stained glass, then walked out into the whispering rain and the empty streets.

***

Where *was* everyone? The question had been vexing me since our train trip from Nantes the previous day. Granted, this was France in August. Many of the locals might have gone to the beach for their own summer holidays. My previous experiences of France – at least since a school exchange to Brittany from which all I could remember was the bowls of hot chocolate we drank for breakfast – had been of Paris. Paris the romantic; Paris the historic; Paris the artistic; and, above all, Paris the hectic, crowded capital, where waiters hurry you out of your restaurant seats because they can see more trade passing by, and where the zebra crossings are there not to enable pedestrians to cross, but to help motorists to achieve the city's quota of hit-and-run accidents. My conditioning meant that I equated 'France' with 'huge numbers of people, everywhere'.

As a commuter to London for many years, Helen had become used to standing up on the train throughout her journey, there or back. So, as we sat in Nantes station listening to the announcements – all preceded with what sounded like the first three notes of *Love and Marriage* – we feared the worst.

The Cholet train was as close as made no difference to a ghost train. When I got bored with reclining on the immaculate *banquette*-like seats, I wandered the length of the train, counting a massive 22 other passengers. The ticket inspector, a ponytailed blonde in her twenties, was not a graduate of the Parisian school of rude service. Even though we hadn't done whatever inexplicable things French people do to their rail tickets (I think we were supposed to put them in a perforating machine on the platform), she smiled and wished us *bon voyage*. We sat back, relaxed and looked forward to a gentle walk through the one and a half kilometres of Cholet that would take us to our hotel.

The problem was that it was the longest one and a half kilometres ever. The first part was fine; we left the station and wandered southwards. But then we consulted a map we'd printed from the great god Internet the night before. We didn't stop and ask at the tourist information centre. Before we knew it, we'd taken a left turn instead of a right. The walk had turned into a trudge by the side of a multi-lane ring road, with the sight of multistorey tower blocks mocking us in the distance. Our bright and breezy conversation had degenerated into comments on the road markings for cycle lanes, which resembled the chalk drawings you see in TV depictions of crime scenes:

'Look, it's a cyclist who's been murdered!'

'That's another one. Someone's killed several of them by the look of it.'

'It must have been a cycle-path.'

The only consolation was that none of the hotels in the town centre looked that inviting. We staggered onto Rue de Napoleon and I wondered if this was what the retreat from Moscow felt like. As my weary gaze fell upon the next street sign, for Rue de Coubertin, I thought we could be pioneering a new Olympic event: long-distance synchronised suitcase-wheeling – like synchronised swimming, but with fewer people… and without the swimming costumes… and the water (unless it began to rain – please don't let it rain). I was lost in France, without enjoying it as much as Bonnie Tyler did.

At last, a police station came into view and a friendly policeman put us right. After two hours on a one and a half kilometre walk, we reached the hotel. I hadn't realised that it would be in Cholet's commercial district, lurking behind an out-of-town McDonald's, a fruit and vegetable hypermarket, a DIY store and a café masquerading as a windmill. Cholet's main hospital was opposite, and the hotel reception area boasted a defibrillator. If it all became too much, I could relax in the knowledge that this was a superb place for a non-fatal heart attack. As it was, nothing of the sort happened; as John Wayne might have said, it was all too quiet.

***

We meandered through the somnolent streets of Cholet. A smiling Choletian middle-aged woman in a red top had pointed us towards a café for small but intense cups of coffee and hot chocolate. After the fiasco of my inadequate navigation from the station to the hotel, Helen had decided to take the precaution of getting a town map from the tourist office. Francois – a short man in his thirties, with a neat shirt and slacks and not-so-neat curly hair – seemed bemused at the prospect of British tourists, but he had provided the map and some advice on the sights of the town.

We were heading for one of the highlights, in the north of Cholet, through a residential quarter, the bins in a line outside the front doors like a guard of honour. Then a large ginger cat sneaked out from behind a bin and settled himself in a patch of front garden. It was the first sign of life for ages.

'Aha!' I said, trying to inject a note of excitement into what was a dull walk. I stopped and racked my brains for one of the two French phrases I could remember from school. By a small miracle, I found it.

'*Le chat... est dans le jardin,*' I concluded in triumph.

'Yes, dear,' said Helen, without breaking stride. She had never been as enthusiastic about cats as me, and a French cat wasn't going to change that.

The cat itself regarded the interlopers with indifference, as cats do. I couldn't think of the French for 'I've got a nice tasty piece of tuna for you', which would have been misleading in any case, so I fell back on: '*Vous êtes un chat très grand.*'

Monsieur Grandchat said nothing. He was a cat without chat. I walked on, wondering whether there would be an opportunity to use the other French phrase from my school days. But it seemed unlikely that the circumstances would arise in which an enquiry about the location of the pen of my aunt would be relevant.

Not to worry - we had now arrived at one of the highlights of Cholet, according to Francois: the textiles museum. Cholet used to be famous for manufacturing lace, handkerchiefs in particular. There is a series of redbrick buildings, with copious examples of the machinery that used to handle the various stages of textile production: spinning, bleaching, weaving and so on. Outside was a garden containing plants connected to the textile industry, such as flax and marigolds, which were used for dyes. The wall displays included group photographs of the people who used to work there, a hundred years ago and more: one photo of men, one for women. Nobody smiled or, if the men did, they hid it beneath thickets of beards and moustaches that were, if anything, more anachronistic than the machines.

The museum had – we were told - revived handkerchief production in Cholet, but the machines were not operational. I wear cotton, but have no idea how it works: the machinery might as well have been instrumentation for torture. I could imagine getting my tie stuck and being dragged to a horrible demise.

Even allowing for the emptiness of the museum and the rain outside, the atmosphere was flat. After a while, I concluded that this might be because I was expecting the wrong things. It was just a safe, old-fashioned museum where people came, looked at objects and read information displays on walls. Museum visitors in the West in recent years have grown spoilt by having so much to do: buttons to press, dinosaur skeletons to climb inside, starship bridges on which to stand and command galactic fleets. This, on the other hand, was not so much low-tech as no tech. You didn't have so much as an audio guide.

Things got more interactive at the other highlight Francois had mentioned, the Art and History Museum. I enjoy art galleries. You can sit and look at the art; or you can sit and have a think; or you can just sit. Or you can pretend to be an art critic. It was a shame I'd forgotten to pack my fake art critic goatee beard. These are fun and easy to use:

1. You stick them on your chin.
2. You go to an art gallery.
3. You stand in front of an exhibit, frown and say something like: 'Ah yes, the atonality of the aesthetic reminds us of the futility of mortality.'

That's how things are in the standard, vanilla art gallery. But this time, even Cholet's Art and History Museum has joined the cult of interactivity, with a Labyrinth. This, said the caption at the start, was 'unique in France' and 'it is forbidden not to take part'. That told us. The Labyrinth was a sequence of rooms: one in darkness with distorting mirrors confusing your sense of direction; another with multicoloured cobwebs; another with walls of flashing light bulbs; and another with psychedelic hypnotic black and white swirls growing and shrinking in front of you. It made for an excellent example of 1960s art and should have come with a free packet of aspirins.

The rest of the place was more conventional. Aside from its fame for lace and red handkerchiefs, Cholet also found fame as a battleground during the Vendee Wars of 1793-6, when Catholics and Royalists mounted an attempt at counterrevolution against the new French Republicans. The forces of revolution under the eye of the Committee for Public Safety – ironic name, that – won the day in the end, and the new regime was secure.

The Art and History Museum houses many full-length portraits of the men who led their fellow Frenchmen into battle. To coin the phrase about English Cavaliers in our own civil war, the men in the paintings all looked Wrong but Romantic, with silk cummerbunds around their waists, sashes round their shoulders, medals on their chests, knee-length boots planted on the ground and one arm pointing to the sky, while holding a hat. It must have taken them ages to get dressed for all that. French style and chic is fine, but what if the battle's over and you're still putting your eyeliner on?

They seemed to like their military heroes. The reception area had a small display devoted to Roland Garros, the aviator and World War I ace, who earned his pilot's licence in Cholet a hundred years ago. He may be the only aviator to have a tennis stadium (in Paris) and an airport (in Reunion) named after him.

It all added to the impression that not a lot goes on in Cholet these days. French art is fun, though, and I hadn't seen the Fabergé eggs yet…

***

In these straitened economic times, a little luxury helps to see us through. Even so, I wasn't expecting to see Fabergé eggs in the middle of a French local festival, sitting on a plush red tablecloth.

The artists had poured their souls, their creative essences, into making these *objets d'art*. I scratched my chin, cursing myself for forgetting my fake art critic goatee beard and my *Dictionary of Arty Phrases*. Each egg's painting portrayed a different scene. Two baby elephants huddled either side of their mother for comfort. A horse stared out, its neck at an angle as if to say: 'This is my best side.' A rural Mediterranean village glistened under a blue sky. Ostriches wandered through fields of green.

Ostriches… Wait a minute. That wasn't right. I'd been to the Kremlin, years ago, and viewed its array of treasures, including some Fabergé eggs. Their intricate beauty didn't include paintings of elephants or horses or villages or ostriches. Above the bench on which the red tablecloth provided its smart backdrop was a sign: 'Ostrich Eggs for sale.'

I sighed, relieved to have escaped entrapment in such an elaborate scam. Why didn't the sellers focus on the real benefits of ostrich eggs? A museum attendant in Berat,

Albania had told me that ostrich eggs were an effective method of keeping spiders away. The spiders thought the eggs were massive spiders, he said. For anyone who doesn't like spiders, like me, that's a massive benefit: ostrich eggs as a spider-exclusive lifestyle choice. Also, of course, eating an ostrich egg is the egg equivalent of the modern fruit injunction of 'five a day'... even if you need a sledgehammer to break the egg and baguettes for your egg soldiers.

Helen and I were 12 kilometres outside the centre of Cholet, at the town's annual 'Festival of Rural Traditions and Deliciousness'. Given Madame Cholet's role as the Wombles' cook, it seemed like the thing to do. We'd been to see the origins of the lace from which her frilly apron and hat might have been made, so now it was time to take a culinary turn.

We'd had a taste of things to come, the previous day, at the town's weekly market. There had been some curiosities: peaches and nectarines flattened into doughnut shapes, for example, some chickens with heads and feet still attached and one stall selling small model dogs. The butchers had perfected their techniques of maintaining eye contact with customers during conversations, while hacking meat to bits to fulfil the orders. One was in holiday mood, if the large pink fluffy toy pig on his counter was anything to go by. Other stalls were closed, their owners no doubt gone to the beach for a couple of weeks.

Now, with the help of a taxi driver who used our journey from the town centre to give his brakes a series of late tests, we were at the big event. The location was a clearing in the middle of pine and oak trees, deep in a campsite. Down the hill, guests who wanted a camping holiday without the camping were enjoying their late morning coffees at a hotel, or thinking about lunch at the lakeside café, while their children went canoeing in the lake and sat on swings in the playground.

The event had been billed as lasting all day. In strict literal terms this was true, in that it took all morning to set things up and the visitors drifted in around lunchtime. Men drew up in small white vans, opened the back doors, picked up small goats by their horns and deposited them in pens at one end of the clearing. The goats were not too happy to be there, judging by the amount of noise they made as they were manhandled – goat-handled? – out of the vans.

In a neighbouring pen, an Aylesbury duck eyed two chickens with suspicion as a black rabbit hurtled out from under a bale of straw. Two small pink pigs nibbled at the grass in the next pen in the line. They might not have been aware that six of their ex-fellow porcines were turning on spits close by, in preparation for a starring role in the pig roast lunch.

Trestle tables and benches sat in the middle of the clearing and a small stage and a large sound system took shape in front of them. The speakers loomed like a technological Stonehenge. As the sun rose to its midday peak, the gaps filled in. Stallholders arrived and assembled their displays of wares. They moved with a quintessential French shrug of an attitude: they were here for the day, so what the hell? If nobody liked their food, the animals could have it. One stall was the exception: an earnest information display on 'agriculture et energie', dispensing advice on solar panels.

Then came the punters – most of them families, some in three generations. They queued in their dozens for a pig roast lunch. Helen and I sneaked forwards, trying not to look too hungry. The lunch, in a white plastic tray with multiple compartments of the type you get on planes, was green salad, white beans, coleslaw, pork, bread and yoghurt. The caterers had managed the feat of converting an attractive-looking collection of pork on the spit into something... not very attractive.

I confined myself to trying an apple fritter from one of the other stalls. But the locals liked their pork roast; they were wolfing lunch down, as a blonde in a black sleeveless top and leggings, with a male backing guitarist, ripped into some middle-of-the-road-sounding French pop. A large man in Barbour jacket and white trousers, greying hair parted in the middle, dashed between the trestle tables acting as MC. He interviewed people and, for his party turn, performed what appeared to be a live version of *Play your Cards Right*. If you correctly guessed either the colour of the next card or whether it was higher or lower, you won a cheap-looking card table mat.

This was not the only opportunity to win things. Anyone who's been to a garden party, a church fete or the like is familiar with the 'guess the weight' competition. You admire the homemade cake, or the jar of sweets, and you write down your best estimate of its weight. If your guess is closest, you win it. Cholet had a variation on this: 'guess the weight of the donkey'.

Katy2 – that was the donkey's name – was in the custody of another man who was built for comfort rather than speed, his girth made more obvious by the pattern of white hoops on his black polo shirt. *'Je m'appelle Katy2,'* said the piece of paper on Katy2's back. *'Devinez combien je pese pour 1 Euro.'* Katy2 would have weighed rather more if she could have got her teeth into the enticing bunch of carrots that her escort held in one hand. Round and round they went, donkey and owner in an absurd *pas de deux*, Katy2 lusting after carrots and the polo-shirted man keeping them out of her reach while he chatted with anyone nearby.

In what I hoped was inconspicuous fashion, I took out my camera phone and started to take pictures of this remarkable beast (and Katy2). The donkey didn't mind; she was focusing on carrots. Monsieur Polo Shirt got a little shirty. He said nothing, but tried to turn himself and

Katy2 the donkey and her owner

Katy2 away without being rude in too obvious a manner. He was still talking to visitors, as he and Katy2 revolved and I revolved with them, like a circle in a spiral, like a wheel within a wheel. We could have been a performance installation back in the town's art gallery.

All the while my mind seethed with questions. If you guessed the closest to Katy2's weight, did you win her? How would we get her home? Or would we just use her to get from our hotel to Cholet station, in all probability quicker than the reverse journey? If this was Katy2, what happened to Katy1? Did someone win her? Monsieur Polo Shirt did not want to communicate with me, so I might never know.

Nor was this the only competition in the festival. As well as providing a showcase for local food, a selection of tractors sat in the clearing, for the admiration of men of a certain age. One of them – a huge monster with terracotta body and hubcaps – had a piece of paper attached: '*Je suis un Som 35. Gagnez moi pour 2 Euros.*'

This was, if anything, a more attractive prospect than Katy2, endearing as she was. By now, our observations had confirmed that French drivers in Cholet did not differ from French drivers in Paris, in their need for speed and their refusal to pay attention to such trivialities as traffic lights, indicators or pedestrians.

If I were going to drive in France, a tractor might be just the thing. The modern-day charioteers of France would think twice before ramming into the back of a tractor. I had no idea whether the tractor or Katy2 would win a drag race. The dream scenario could be to win them both, and sit on the tractor as Katy2 pulled us through the Channel Tunnel and home. Neither would fit within our limit of one item of hand baggage each for the return flight; that was for certain. With a certain amount of regret, but aware of the difficulties that could occur, I forbore from taking any risk of winning Katy2 or the Som 35.

Cholet, it seemed, had all the eccentricity of its Womble namesake, but less culinary skill. My next Wombles journeys would be closer to home, back in England…

A PAIR OF
WELLINGTONS

'When's it starting?' asked the woman in the Day-Glo hair and the peach Melba fairy skirt.

Her male companion's verdict was concise: 'Late, probably.'

It seemed he was right. I'd been walking up the main street for ages, as a sunny afternoon dimmed into early evening, and the big event was nowhere in sight. I had made the opposite journey in the car the previous lunchtime, zooming down the M4 and M5 into Somerset before turning off for Wellington. Car-crawling down the High Street to my B&B had taken longer than walking.

'That'll be the shift changes at the factory,' the stout lady in the town museum had told me that afternoon. 'They change shifts at lunchtime on Fridays – it's a half day for folks who work there. So they come off shift and get into town to do their shopping.'

What did the factories produce?

'Beds,' she told me. 'Beds and aerosols.'

For some reason I found this answer depressing. Somebody has to manufacture beds and aerosols, of course. But did it have to be Wellington – the town that gave its name to bespectacled, school cap-wearing, aspiring scientist Wellington Womble? I had hoped for something more exciting or unusual.

Now I was trudging back uphill, from the old vicarage in Rockwell Green where I was staying to the top of the high street, to witness the annual Carnival, part of a county-wide programme of carnivals which the organisers described as 'the largest illuminated procession in the world'.

My landlady had smiled: 'Oh, yes, you can see some of the carnivals from space!'

So far, the most excitable local had been a large Alsatian, sitting with its front paws on a garden wall, a red plastic ball in its mouth and a nonchalant expression on its face as I took its photo.

'I'm a dog with a ball – so what?' it might have been saying, if its mouth hadn't been full of ball.

People were, nonetheless, starting to line the road on both sides, in anticipation of the evening's events. Families of up to three generations scrambled for places, with the grandmothers settling themselves in little deckchairs, in the narrow gaps between the cars whose drivers had done their best to get bumper to bumper.

Some were queuing at mobile kiosks for their preferred permutation of sausage, pork, chips, beans and candyfloss. Others admired the wares of the entrepreneurs walking up and down the centre of the road. Apart from balloons, the entire stock consisted of items that glowed: simple sticks, sticks with skulls on them, light sabres and horns that made a piercing single note. Perhaps the spectators, rather than the processions, illuminated the carnival?

'Oh, no, don't worry, it'll be all lit up tonight!' said a petite blonde in a fluorescent yellow jacket which indicated her status as one of the safety marshals. 'Some of the floats are like one-man National Grids… you won't miss them. They're the ones with the most sponsorship.'

I continued walking, past the small Chinese takeaway on the left, past the 1930s-style Wellesley cinema on the right. Within a few minutes I had passed more people than there had been in the Wellesley the previous evening (this was not difficult, as the total audience for the film was nine, and that was down to two last minute rushes). Less than ten minutes before the start of the programme, I stood in the dusk on the steps of the entrance.

The first last minute rush was a one-man operation. He wore a leather jacket, jeans straining at the seams and a bored expression.

'At least it's not just me then,' I ventured.

He looked embarrassed.

'Well, actually... it is. I'm an auditor. I'm only here to make sure that the adverts that are supposed to be shown get shown. Then I'm off!'

The doors opened, the cinema's extensive staff (one) stamped our tickets and sold us (me) ice cream, and we settled in our seats. The second last minute rush was more convincing – another seven people, six of them in pairs, including a middle-aged or older couple of women. One of the pair talked throughout the ads on a broad range of topics including how to poach eggs, personal attendants and myriad other things. The acoustics of an empty cinema meant we could hear every word. She didn't seem to notice or mind. The only thing missing was Alan Bennett, to turn it into a play.

Goodness knew where everybody else had been then; they were lining Wellington's main street now, eating their snacks, waving their light sabres and gossiping with their neighbours. A few of the locals might have wandered out of the screen from the night before. The film, about a sleepy village thrown into chaos by the return of a local girl who has made good as a journalist, featured two local girls with typical big-screen West Country 'local yokel' accents. Several pairs of their real life equivalents strolled past me, talking at 100 miles an hour, with the occasional pause to consult text messages and exclaim: 'Oh! My! GOD!'

Others were hanging out of the windows of offices overlooking the high street, as night began to fall. Even at first floor level, the illuminations were in use, as girls wore fluorescent rabbit ears as their fashion item of choice. Two of them watched as a teenager came off shift from the local supermarket, bearing packets of cookies in each hand.

'Oi! Waitrose! Come over here with those cookies!'

He looked up at the source of the shouts, giggled and replied: 'Well, there's two cookies with your names on them here if you come down for them!'

I walked on, past the assignations and the men standing, looking uncertain, outside three-quarters-empty pubs, pints in hands. By now, a van had arrived opposite the post office as the base for announcements throughout the procession.

'Now remember, ladies and gentlemen, we don't need any more accidents than strictly necessary...'

I wondered how many accidents were strictly necessary.

'So make sure the little ones stay well back from the road. Every float you see tonight is advertising local businesses and especially local charities. I know times are hard, but please, please do find those extra pennies. Every penny helps...'

The smells of candyfloss and onions and sausages and chips and ketchup wafted along, as the light sabre traders wheeled their wares up and down the street, shouting incomprehensible offers of discounts. Then they dispersed as police vans, ambulances and St John's Ambulance officers on bikes all made their way uphill along the high street. At last, the big event was here.

Not that it seemed that big, to start with. Miss Wellington and Miss Junior Wellington (with their 'lady-in-waiting') waved in gracious style from the back of the long vehicle transporting them. A tractor with DOMINO emblazoned in lights across its front bumper rumbled past, followed by a van advertising the wonders of Wookey Hole, which was towing a cage with a large, angry-looking tyrannosaurus rex. The Wellington Majorettes, in their purple blazers and white skirts, twirled their batons and skipped along.

'Don't worry, folks, the big guns are on their way,' boomed the PA. When someone mentions guns in a town named Wellington, it's a nervous moment.

But the PA meant big floats, not big guns: and big floats with plenty of light. I'd read that some carnival floats used up to 30,000 light bulbs. As a medieval castle came towards us, complete with costumed knights and damsels gyrating to Bee Gees music - *(K)night Fever*, if you must ask – it became clearer what my B&B landlady had meant.

That afternoon I had visited Wellington's Lighting Company, situated at the southern end of the high street in an old church. It reminded me of the supermarket inhabiting an old church in Tobermory.

'We've been here a few years,' said the Lighting Company shop manager. 'It used to be an auction room before this. It's a wonderful space in which to demonstrate lighting solutions.'

Not even a reused church could have housed some of the marvels thundering up the high street. An entrant to the carnival with enough time and money could select any theme for their display. 'Gepetto's Workshop', featuring a giant moustachioed figure along the lines of Pinocchio's creator, was so impressive I forgot to check whose float it was. Then it was the turn of Rome, another blaze of electric light heralding a display of centurions, foot soldiers and a bored-looking (stuffed) tiger. 'Over the Rainbow' featured, as you might expect, Dorothy, a tin man and a lion… and so on, for what seemed like a very long time indeed. The general rule was: the bigger and more extravagant the float, the louder the accompanying music.

The crowds liked it: grannies moved their deckchairs (or wheelchairs) to the edges of the pavements, while toddlers waved their light sabres and cheered. Carnival marshals kept spectators off the road as best they could, while judges with serious-looking clipboards furrowed their brows and thought about who would win the big prize of the evening, for most impressive float. At long last the floats disappeared out of view, heading for a roundabout nearer Taunton than Wellington where, hours later, the prize winners' identities would be announced.

At the back of many of the floats and costumed characters – including a very irritated-looking Henry VIII - was a space into which the crowds could throw their loose change and hence make donations to charitable causes. Members of the local cadet forces walked behind, picking up coins as they fell in the road. At some point – about halfway through the procession – the small boys either side of me in the crowd decided that it was more fun to throw the coins at the cadets than into the floats. To the relief of the local hospital, no doubt, their aims were far from perfect, and nobody lost an eye from a spare copper coin.

How the local lighting company would have loved to provide all the bulbs for this event. Celebrations are celebrations, and this was the biggest event of Wellington's year, a venerable local tradition. With the best will in the world, you couldn't call it energy efficient.

***

The other main event in town that day was more people-intensive than light-bulb-laden. There was an Open Morning for prospective pupils and parents at Wellington School.

The school itself nestled in a mix of old and new buildings either side of South Street, with the opening remarks from the head teacher in a presentation room – albeit with old-fashioned lectern – in one of the newer buildings, which from the outside could have passed for a DIY store. The head teacher, with his grey hair over a youthful face, smart black suit, blue shirt and red tie, bore an uncomfortable resemblance to Tony Blair. I half-expected him to declare that he was tough on students and tough on the causes of students.

In fact, he was at pains to stress the 'family atmosphere' – something which, he said, could be observed by the frequency with which pupils greeted their teachers with a 'Hi, Sir' or 'Hi, Miss' – and the good quality, without needless glitz, of the teaching facilities. His theme was 'Affordable Excellence'.

Behind the head teacher's audience, at the back of the room, was a small suited and booted army of staff and pupils. The older students – between the ages of sixteen and eighteen – were so smart that they might have passed for junior staff. As visitors moved out of the room, clutching prospectuses in one hand and chocolate biscuits or drinks in the other, we were all assigned a guide, who would take us round whatever we wanted to see and answer any questions.

'Ask them anything you like,' the head teacher had encouraged us. 'I've given you the official spiel but they can give you the student's perspective.'

My guide was Tom, a pupil from year 7 – which in English meant he was ten years old. Tom wore a navy blue blazer, a blue and black striped tie and facial expressions which defaulted somewhere between serious and nervous. I am not tall, but Tom's head seemed to be at the level of my knee. If Wellington Womble had taken human form, Tom could have been the result.

We embarked on a brisk, hour-long tour, hopping back and forth across South Street. Tom started me off with the art department. My two years of studying art at secondary school ended, as football clubs and their managers now put it, by mutual consent (I was useless), so anyone who can draw, paint, sculpt, work with wood, work with metal, take photographs or do anything artistic at all is ahead of me. Tom was keen on art, but not yet full of faux art-speak. When I asked him about the thought processes behind a blue collage which he and other pupils had created, he looked at me for a moment and said: 'I don't know. We just did it.' He pointed out some excellent drawings of owls by a friend of his.

The lunch hall housed a photographic exhibition, including one image by Tom - of a pile of flying fish – which had won a runner-up prize in a school competition.

'I took it in Barbados where my uncle lives. I like to fill the frame with pictures,' he said with a shy smile. 'There was another picture which I took by sitting near some waves just as they were cresting. I had to be brave!'

In some schools, including mine, pupils such as Tom would have shown visitors their own artwork and photos first. I found his modesty refreshing.

Next stop was the chapel, whose conventional design was offset by a shiny, coral-blue patterned floor, as if the choir and congregation were gathering at the bottom of a swimming pool. This was a good place to come, Tom said.

I made a confession; my family background is Jewish, so where would I or my children worship? Would they have to sit in services in silence? Tom looked uncertain; this question, it was clear, was not in the briefing notes he clutched in one hand.

'Well… they wouldn't have to join in. They could just come in for the service and not sing. There's about 8% of the pupils from overseas, so I expect some of them aren't Christian.'

Tom had borrowed this statistic from the head teacher's earlier speech. As it happened, his own family's roots were from overseas, too: the Faroe Islands, before 'Granny came down south with a man in the [second world] war'.

I asked to see the science facilities, to test just how much of a Wellington Tom was. He was an endearing blend of confidence and diffidence, bounding up and down stairs two steps at a time, but sucking the end of his tie in agitation if any crowd of people threatened to bar our way through.

'I'm not that good at anything,' he said, as we passed the rugby pitch where shivering boys were warming up for a match with a team from another school. Tom wanted, he said, to be a doctor. He seemed quieter than some of his fellow pupils whom we found demonstrating experiments in the chemistry laboratories, mostly with test tubes and Bunsen burners. One boy was showing 'what happens when you eat magnesium, which I don't think is a good idea.'

Like the biology and design technology spaces, the chemistry labs had an air of smartness without ostentation. The exception to this was the resident teacher, whose white coat had students' names written in (ineradicable?) ink of various colours.

'It's the easiest way for me to remember who they all are. This helps me to remember them all, it's my portable register!'

So what happened when he ran out of space on the coat? 'I get a new coat!'

We moved on to the sports hall. Fencing, trampolining and table tennis were taking place in three sections of the main hall. Tom became quite animated on the difference between épée, foil and sabre – 'you can tell from the blades, they each have their own shape'. The fencing teacher had once been an Olympian, representing Hungary.

On the way out, my eye fell on the inevitable rows of team photographs from years and decades past. Tom must have been surprised that I was so interested in the older photos.

'The newer ones are in colour,' he pointed out. 'Even though it isn't very good colour.'

He was bemused, though, when I observed how long the boys' hair had been in the 1970s. Long hair for boys was not something Tom had yet come across.

Once he had returned me to the original presentation room, Tom shook my hand and moved off in a discreet beeline for the chocolate biscuits and fruit juice. Considering his age, the experience of guiding someone like me around the school for an hour, and answering my inane questions, must have been quite an ordeal. He had managed to show a stranger some of the school's highlights, and some of his own interests and enthusiasm, without boasting.

The school's famous old boys, according to Wellington Museum, included the author and sometime political dilettante Jeffrey Archer, the late chef and raconteur Keith Floyd and the actor David Suchet. Tom had exhibited neither the flair nor (in the first two cases) the propensity for tall tales of his famous predecessors, but I was impressed. He had been a worthy Wellington guide.

***

Sometimes, our means of escape becomes a prison cell.

Such a place exists in another Wellington in Shropshire. The cell's outward form is that of a bookshop. The books squeeze onto the shelves, more sit at the foot of the bookcases and others spill out into the street. The legend 'Books bought' in the window is optimistic; where there's space, there will soon be books, it seems.

Sitting in the far left corner, about the length of my living room away from the entrance, is the owner/manager. He wears a blazer, smart trousers, a white shirt and a tie with red and blue stripes of meaningful affiliation. Below the salt and pepper hair is a grave, tired expression. So this is where Dirk Bogarde has got to.

Another man is sitting in chair opposite Dirk, with his back to the entrance, while a third stands by the desk. Fractions of conversation float around as I browse:

'How many famous Latvians are there, compared to famous Austrians?'

'Ah, yes, the Austrians. Without Austria there is no civilisation.'

The etiquette of browsing in second-hand bookshops dictates that you do not, on any account, join in such a conversation. You continue to browse. So that's what I do.

After a few minutes, the seated visitor leaves, while the other stays and takes his seat. Dirk lowers his voice and I only catch snatches: 'You see what I have to put up with... lunatic... sheer lunatic.'

After a time, the second visitor leaves. Dirk peers round a bookcase at me.

'Can I help you at all?'

'Oh well, I'm just browsing.'

I find a novel by someone more famous for their science fiction writings.

Dirk smirks: 'Ah, science fiction is something of a blank to me.'

Most of literature is a blank to me, I reply.

Dirk muses: 'Ah, well, which of us is more bereft?'

The conversation continues, except for moments when I duck out of sight behind a bookcase, at which point Dirk pauses until I'm in his sights again. Dirk, it turns out, used to work in London, as a specialist writer 'on petroleum'. After more than 30 years, he moved to Wellington and acquired the bookshop.

'I haven't drunk nearly as much since moving.'

We talk about cars for a while. He notices my Alfa Romeo key ring.

'Ah – you're a sportsman?'

I shake my head.

'One of the Italian models used to have a channel down the centre of the car, from the back to the front, to store your skis. But I heard from a friend of a friend that Mafia types used it to store their rifles.'

Dirk seems to like his conversations with visitors, whether they buy books or not. Since the start of the year, he has kept a book of visitors' comments. There are over two dozen entries, ranging from 'This shop is kool' (by a teenager) to a short essay on the 'intellectual and strategic significance' of the name of the shop. I settle for 'excellent eclecticism'.

'You can't read Greek, can you?' asks Dirk. I can't. At least three entries, written in Greek, will remain a mystery to him and me.

Dirk inspects the books I have chosen, which include one of Jan Morris's works.

'Ah, yes,' he approves. 'Jan Morris – a fine writer.'

'Yes,' I say. 'Probably the greatest living Welsh republican transsexual travel writer.'

Dirk moves the conversation on.

'I've had a dangerous morning,' he confides, lowering his voice again although nobody else is in the shop.

I try to look as neutral as possible. Danger, in a bookshop?

'You probably noticed him in here when you first came in… a man in a big leather coat, with a Mohican-style haircut. I sold him a copy of *The Satanic Verses* a while ago. He came in today to *demand* that I sell him another copy, with a blue cover. Apparently some local occult group has put a curse on him, for some reason.

'He grasped my wrist – like this, you see? - and wanted the blue edition… I don't have a blue edition. The trouble is I'm trapped in here... on the street I would have crossed the road. Perhaps you saw the other gentleman in here with him? He tells me he is that man's psychiatric counsellor. He gave me all sorts of personal details about him. Appropriate details, professional details, of course.'

If the man's counsellor is keeping a close eye on him, that's reassuring, I suggest.

'Not entirely… I've found out that I'm not personally insured in here. The property is insured, the books and the contents are insured if anything happens… but if someone comes in and stabs me, nothing. According to Norwich Union, or whatever they call themselves now.'

Strange as it seems for a quiet little place like Wellington, Shropshire, this is the second mention of *The Satanic Verses* I have heard today...

***

I'd been looking forward to meeting Harry, a local historian. He had responded to my initial enquiry by email:

'Our Wellington has nothing to do with the Iron Duke and we don't make rubber boots. We have a few techies but don't have a lot of scientists, not even nerds. I think we may be the oldest and second largest Wellington (after New Zealand). I have only been here for 87 years so only know a little. Friends say Wellington's history is what I remember and the bits I made up. I will be happy to meet you.'

Before meeting Harry, I explored the small town centre. It was a twenty minute walk from the hotel, though the receptionist's expression suggested that might just as well be twenty days. I strolled past redbrick schools and Chinese 'walk-in supermarkets' (as if to differentiate them from the supermarkets where you stand in the doorway and negotiate through intermediaries). Wellington abounded in charity shops, whether for people in need or for 'pets who need vets'. Some early modern architecture survived, in the form of pubs. One went by the name of Rasputin, though the pub sign of a tonsured monk, holding a yellow duck while licking his lips, did not resemble the famous Russian, as far as I could see. The building had been a hotel before its change of use.

'*Why change?*' Harry had written, ten years ago. '*Presumably this ancient and once respectable inn, a listed building, is about to become trendy and tacky. Pity. With any luck it will return to its former self when the brashness wears off.* Not being in need of brashness, trendiness or tackiness, I avoided going inside.

Although dust was blowing up from building works, the Shropshire Wellington was a tidy, well-behaved place. The parents should take some credit. A little boy, no more than five years old, dropped his drink in the street as I watched, and refused to pick it up despite his mother's instructions.

'I can't drink it,' he insisted.

His father told him: 'Well, throw it away then. Go on – the bin's over there.'

In slow and reluctant fashion, the boy disposed of his drink. A girl of around the same age sat outside a supermarket, staring at a nearby pigeon. Her mother told her, 'No, we aren't going to smash that little bird on the head. Now put your glasses on.' The pigeon remained, unmolested.

On the drive from the town centre towards Harry's house, I stopped for petrol. The cashier, a middle-aged brunette, looked up from her till and said: 'Aaaaah!' I don't tend to get that reaction from people, and petrol station cashiers are not famous for greeting their customers with fondness. She was reacting not to me, but to Wellington, who was sitting in my top pocket.

'So you've heard of the Wombles?' I asked.

'Oh, yes, of course. Is that Great Uncle Bulgaria?'

I paid the bill and drove on.

Harry had written many books on Wellington and its history; its millennium, its living landscape, its markets and its walks. Harry was keen for the locals to shop in the markets, rather than going elsewhere. He wrote: 'There is a hidden agenda which I should confess. I do not apologise for the fact that I am very fond indeed of my town. So one of the most important reasons for writing this book is to try to persuade people to enjoy this interesting place as much as I do.'

Harry described himself as 'an old optimist' and his home town as 'increasingly a place of students, of take-away food and of small computer shops… a good place to live.' Telford had been 'inflicted' on East Shropshire, but Harry believed that Wellington was 'a distinct, special place.'

His writing included some namedropping; Charles I, Kenneth Horne and Oswald Mosley had passed through the town, and Larkin Way got its name from '*our former librarian, internationally acclaimed poet and well known local grouch, Philip Larkin*'. But I preferred Harry's personal reminiscences about some old places and characters he had known:

'Bert Richards was a hairdresser and tobacconist, so, as was traditional, he sold umbrellas. Please don't ask why… The "pop" works was originally built as a brewery but was sold on condition that no brewing took place on the premises… [in the old market] There was a trader who sold crockery and used to loudly break some to attract attention. There was an old woman who sold cheese and would gouge you a sample out with her filthy black thumb nail.'

By the time I wandered up the driveway of Harry's house, I was looking forward to meeting this wise old man with a twinkle in his eye. He smiled, gave me a firm handshake and ushered me into his study for a cup of tea and a biscuit.

Harry looked the part. People tend to shrink as they age, but he was still of medium height and bald with a white beard. Three layers – a white vest, green shirt and gingham patterned blue and white over-shirt – protected him from the elements, although this was a warm and sunny spring day.

Some pets resemble their owners. Harry's study took after him: comfortable and lived-in. Geographical journals and histories of Shropshire lined one wall;

certificates adorned another. Photos of Harry's wife and of Harry with a group of students (for he had been a teacher) vied for space with an aerial view of the nearby Wrekin, a local hill.

Harry had been born in the room over his father's furniture shop – '1923 if you must know'. His father had started working life as a farmer. 'Then he decided, for some reason, he wanted to sell furniture, after coming back from the "war to end all wars" (World War I). He went back to farming, and eventually became a foreman in a factory making rubber ducks!'

I studied the certificates. They included a geography degree from the University of London dated 1971, a counselling certificate and a Fellowship of the Royal Geographical Society. Had Harry always been bright?

'Well, I was idle at school, a bit like my eldest son – it's something in the genes! The French master came up to me before the School Certificate and said, "You're going to fail because you'll fail French". To get the Certificate you had to pass English, Maths, a foreign language, a science, and three other subjects. Well, after he said that, I got busy… and passed.'

The improving student was called into the headmaster's study one day.

'He told me that "The only thing you're any good at is geography. And as you don't have enough brains, the thing you need to do is get a job making maps. " I looked into it… and it seemed to consist of holding up poles all day so others could make maps. That didn't seem very fulfilling.'

Harry joined the services, was posted to various places around Britain and Northern Ireland, and celebrated his 21st birthday in 1944… 5 June 1944 to be precise. He got 'paralytically drunk' – just in time for his first trip abroad.

'The next day, with a terrible hangover, I invaded Normandy. We had to jump across from the ship to a landing craft and I was drunk and laden down with a Bren gun and 300 rounds of ammunition. If I'd fallen in the sea I'd have drowned. There was this rope ladder arrangement... anyway I managed it, and got to shore... body parts lying all over the place. And I realised this wasn't playing for fun, this was playing for keeps.'

Those twinkling eyes screwed up tight, as if to see into a terrible past.

'My unit had 70% casualties. But we got through France, Belgium and so on, until we reached Germany and met the Russians coming the other way. We went up to Schleswig-Holstein and managed to stop Admiral Donitz getting any funny ideas about taking over from Hitler. And on 8 May 1945 everyone stopped shooting!'

Harry stayed on in Germany and discovered an aptitude for teaching.

'I started teaching maths and the army said they needed me to teach English. So I took a week's course – it was better than square-bashing – and came out with a certificate, ready to teach English. Then they said I had to teach mathematics! The Army's like that. Stupid buggers!

'I was shown a three storey block of flats and told I had two weeks to open a school for the children staying there. Somehow it opened within two weeks and I got a chitty from the commanding officer to ensure I got anything I needed. I even got promoted from private to sergeant – I was teaching sergeants and they were complaining about being taught by a private.'

Eventually, Harry came back to Wellington. He only went abroad a couple of times since – once to America.

'My son was designing a 1,300 acre garden for an American, in America. Well, we were due to fly home from New York to Manchester, and the day before we flew home was a big air crash. I've never been so terrified. I never understood why planes don't just fall straight down to the ground.'

Fresh from his successes in Germany, Harry got a temporary teaching certificate to work at a local school. His first class was a group of fifty 14-year-old boys.

'The headmaster said: "They've all got Bibles, teach them religious education. Here's a stick in case you need it. " I didn't need it – I just waved it about a bit but didn't use it. We started with psalm 23 (The lord is my shepherd) and went from there. I'd been thrown in the deep end and I managed to swim to the other side.'

Harry enjoyed later life as a geography teacher, including the outdoor excursions when he would take up to 35 boys walking through woods, climbing trees and swimming.

'I was the sole, responsible adult. I used to say to the boys before they swam: "If you drown, I will be very cross." And none of them did.'

His smile didn't waver, but Harry's eyes flicked between their normal twinkle and a forbidding sternness, as he remembered how he used to enforce discipline with any pupils who couldn't or wouldn't toe the line.

'One boy hadn't been paying attention three times in a row, so I held him upside down by one ankle with his head in the waste paper basket! He didn't seem too put out by it. But it worked…

After retiring, I didn't want to be a retired teacher like all the other retired teachers, so I started writing. Even now I write 1000 word columns for the local freebie. *Exactly* 1000 words, mind you.'

On occasions – several occasions – his articles turned into books.

'I was the joint bestselling author in the area with one book – joint bestselling with *The Satanic Verses*!'

And among Harry's remembrances of Wellingtonians past was one William Withering, who was born in 1741, studied at Edinburgh and was a physician at

Birmingham General Hospital from 1775. In 1776, he published *The botanical arrangement of all the vegetables naturally growing in Great Britain*, which continued to be published under various authors until 1877. He carried out pioneering work into the identification of fungi and invented a folding pocket microscope for use on botanical field trips.

But Withering's greatest triumph – so the story goes – was to notice some sufferers of dropsy getting better after taking a traditional herbal remedy, and to recognise the active ingredient originated from foxglove. That ingredient became known as digitalis. Later in his career, Withering worked with, and then fell out with, Erasmus Darwin, grandfather of Charles.

'Ah, yes...' A smile crossed Harry's lips. 'William Withering, the greatest scientist nobody has ever heard of!'

And, I thought wryly, the original scientist from Wellington: with achievements for the aspiring scientist Wellington Womble to aspire to.

When he wasn't writing for the local paper, or turning his articles into books, Harry was campaigning: for Wellington to be recognised as part of The Wrekin, not Shropshire, and to have its own status independent of Telford; for people to shop in their local market; for his own address to include The Wrekin.

'I've never wanted to move. One town is much like another, isn't it? It has people in it and some of them are human. And round here I know which ones! Some teachers prefer to live outside their school's catchment area, they don't want to see the pupils outside school. I was never like that.

'Lots of small towns like Wellington have evolved over the centuries, then *splat*! We get Telford. That's not a town, it's a building site with attitude. Not the people of Telford, they're nice enough. It's the place. I've had a hell of a good time living in Wellington. It's a great place to live – and I think it will be even better in the future.'

Our time was almost up, as Harry had a meeting to go to. I asked him what his top recommendation would be for a visitor spending time in Wellington.

'Oh, that's easy. Go up the Wrekin. Everyone round here does that, and they're all right. It's beautiful. I'll be there tomorrow myself. But please, I'm not being rude but don't come up and say hello. I won't want to know.'

I didn't know what to say. Had I offended him in some way?

'No, no. It's just that I'll be spreading my wife's ashes… she died last November… along with 12 other members of the family who have come up. We'll be having a picnic then coming back here for some beers and so on. We were married for 60 years.'

I looked at the photos around the study, of his wife at various ages. And, inconspicuous in the corner, a framed letter to her from Mrs Thatcher from early 1980.

'Ah, yes… my wife was a local activist. I was on the extreme left of the party. They would have called me a "wet", probably!'

They had been at neighbouring schools, but she was five years Harry's junior. This – along with a 15-foot wall between the schools – ensured they didn't meet until after the war. I apologised for taking Harry's time the day before such an important event.

'That's quite all right. Talking to someone about something else helps to take my mind off it. Tomorrow will be fine. I'm just looking after this house for the family, now.'

His bonhomie reasserted itself as he gave a couple of other books by local authors about Wellington schooldays. I shook his hand in farewell and went to enjoy Wellington and its second-hand bookshops. I took a brisk walk most of the way up the Wrekin, and visited nearby Hoo Farm, where the parrots are loquacious and the goat race was enlivened by at least one goat turning round, halfway through, and going back to the start. It wasn't only the local humans like Harry who had a stubborn streak, then.

That afternoon, in the grounds of All Saints Church, teenagers lolled on the grass, spreading generous daubs of vinegar on their fish and chips. Small children shouted at their parents as they raced between the trees, motorbikes raced past and the pub and Italian restaurant prepared for the evening trade.

I read the preface in one of Harry's books, and his message of thanks to 'my wife, guide, proofreader, adviser, muse, spellchecker, encourager, inspiration, drinks waitress, cook, conscience and interrupter – it would never have happened without you.'

Harry knew how to be brave, curious, cheerful and more. If the younger people of the Shropshire Wellington – and Tim and his friends in Somerset – inherited those qualities, then Harry's optimism for the future would be justified.

It was time for me to leave both Wellingtons behind – and to travel to the Far East...

SHANSI

'Which spelling are you using?'

'Er… is there more than one?'

Phil looked at me, the way people do when you've asked a stupid question, but they don't want to make it obvious.

'That's the trouble with Chinese spellings and transliterations,' he said, all fingers and thumbs and iPhone as he looked it up. Phil was an anthropologist, and he was about to go to China for several months of fieldwork, researching the use of music in small Chinese towns and villages.

'Well,' said Phil, scrolling around the tiny phone screen. 'There are two provinces in the east according to this. One is Shanxi and one is Shaanxi. But there might be an alternative spelling of Shensi or Shenxi.'

My atlas had indicated that Shansi was an old name for one of the western provinces.

'That's possible, too…'

Life was imitating art again. 'People don't notice us, they never see / Under their noses, a Womble may be,' Mike Batt had sung, all those years ago. It seemed that it was also possible to visit places named after Wombles, without knowing it at the time. I'd been through China – and at least two of the Shansi suspects – a few years before, and a strange trip it was, too.

***

The trip had started in Beijing, after five unscheduled hours in a car park in the rain at Heathrow. We had demonstrated the British approach to making pancake rolls (cack-handed), to the consternation of Beijing restaurant staff. We had wondered at the absence of trees in the Forbidden City: our guide Penny told us this was an ancient precaution, to minimise hiding places for would-be assassins.

Penny had shown us how to spot false banknotes, and had taken us for a walk along a quiet part of the Great Wall – a short walk, as I don't like heights and Helen is not keen on steep steps. Penny had shared some local myths and superstitions with us as well.

Pointing to an elderly couple across the road, she said: 'According to tradition, every time a Chinese wife has an affair, another hair turns grey on her husband's head.'

My own grey hairs (which Penny hadn't spotted) are nobody's fault but Nature. Helen and I covered our mouths, trying not to giggle. Great Uncle Bulgaria, whose fur is white but who is neither Chinese nor married, would not have been amused.

Penny was one of a series of guides available to help us at each of our stays as we went west, from Beijing to Kashgar and over the border into Kyrgyzstan and then Uzbekistan. Our train pulled out of Beijing – to the strains of *Auld Lang Syne* which, we were told later in the trip, was 'a traditional Chinese tune'. We were on the way to Xi'an in Shaanxi province (going past Shanxi province, just to confuse the issue), where Iris was waiting for us. She was a short, willowy figure in her matching floral-patterned short-sleeved top and skirt, using a small umbrella to shade herself from the sun.

Iris was studying for a degree in tourism, she told us as we walked around Xi'an's city walls one morning, admiring the red lantern displays and dodging the cyclists.

'I have never been outside China,' said Iris. 'I have never even seen the sea. One day, I would like to go to Europe. I am told it has beautiful beaches.'

We nodded and asked which beaches Iris had in mind for her visit.

'I like the sound of Switzerland,' she said.

As our knowledge of China was likely to be less extensive than Iris's knowledge of Europe, we didn't dissuade her. It did make me wonder what Chinese students learn about us. Later in the trip, our Urumqi guide, on finding that we lived near London, asked: 'How is the smog?' Gone fifty years ago, but thanks for asking.

Iris and the other residents of Xi'an (Xi'anians? that can't be right; it sounds like they should be allied with the Klingons) did have some first-hand knowledge of the West. Opposite the city's Bell Tower sat that symbol of globalisation, a branch of Starbucks. The Chinese can rip off a good idea, which they had done in Xi'an by creating a Starbuck-a-like called King Coffee. My 'blue raspberry cake' was raspberry and chocolate cake, while Helen's 'Kazakh sand cake' was chocolate cake with a cherry on the top. A corner of the Muslim Quarter is a little piece of Britain, too; as we walked there one evening, an Old English Sheepdog took up much of the pavement.

On the other hand, you can have too much adaptation of foreign customs; the main square was enacting a Xi'an version of *Britain's Got Talent*. The bubble machines and fireworks were more entertaining than the humans.

Helen and I were moving slowly that morning. We'd gone to a Tang Dynasty show the night before, a programme of music, song and dance in traditional costumes against a painted set of the Forbidden City. A musician who could make Donald Duck sounds, without instruments, was top of the bill. We might have given him a standing ovation if we hadn't already eaten at the show banquet, which included dumplings with 18 types of filling (chicken, pork, abalone, prawn, pickle, walnut and so on), topped up with soup, meat and peanuts.

Throughout our stay in China, our hosts insisted on supplying enough food for a group of large Americans (who would normally be travelling this route). It was reminiscent of *The Wombles Go Round the World*, in which Bungo and Orinoco take a hot air balloon from east to west while Tomsk and Wellington take another balloon in the opposite direction. Orinoco doesn't get the chance to experience Chinese cuisine, apart from a two-hour feast in San Francisco's Chinatown. Xi'an may be in Shaanxi province but, if places were named after Wombles rather than the other way round, it would be Orinoco province.

In the end, though, there is one thing in Xi'an – or just outside Xi'an – which gives this place world renown...

***

There was never a chance of us leaving Xi'an without paying a visit to the Terracotta Warriors. Local peasants discovered the site in 1974 while digging for a well. The subsequent excavations have found thousands of life-sized armoured soldiers and horses, intended – it is almost certain – to act as bodyguards for the ghost of Qin Shihuangdi, the First Emperor of China.

Qin was born Ying Sheng, the son of the King of Qin, in central China, in 259BC. After becoming king, he used a highly organised army to conquer the neighbouring states. By 221BC, a central core of modern China existed as a single state, with Ying Sheng declaring himself Qin Shihuangdi. Qin oversaw the building of a wall on the northern frontier – farther north than today's Great Wall – and the unification of the currency and the written script. The army represents, in effect, Qin's attempt to ensure a safe and successful passage to the next world. Qin may not have achieved the literal immortality he craved; this is the next best thing.

There are three buildings, each with a vault (or pit), as well as two exhibition halls. Pit One is the largest – it feels like an aircraft hangar – and, if and when excavations are complete, there may be as many as 6,000 warriors down there. Pit Two may contain up to 1,000 warriors, many of them archers – often in firing positions, upright or kneeling. Pit Three may have been the command headquarters, as it is the smallest of the three and only 69 warriors have been uncovered so far.

The pits are lit sufficiently to show their contents without damaging them, which creates a somewhat eerie effect. The warriors themselves boast a wide variety of armour and, for that matter, headgear. Different hats denote different ranks, although the exact details escaped me. They all carried weapons originally. Each individual model was not necessarily an exact copy of a real person; a small range of body parts was produced using moulds, coiling and slab building. A little, but not much, of the original colour remains on some of the bodies. But the most striking aspect is the facial expressions: not aggressive or even fierce; full of calm concentration.

The two bronze chariots on display in the museum are as notable in their own way. One of the keys to the army's success was the improved design of smaller wheels, with more spokes which provided greater stability. The width of axles was made uniform under Qin, enabling chariots to ride in smooth fashion down the same ruts in the road.

As a monument to one man's ego, it is hard to imagine anything more effective than this display - though the sculptors did give the soldiers individuality, which in our modern Photoshopped world is something for which to be grateful.

Coming from Britain where museums are now expected to be interactive – you can't just go into the Natural History Museum, you have to walk through the reconstructed skeleton of a dinosaur to do so – I found the no-tech, no-touch approach refreshing. No video screens; no PA systems booming out instructions, advice or advertising. (I've been sceptical of the power of PA systems since visiting the Sistine Chapel. A huge, God-like voice issued from nowhere: 'Do NOT speak! Do NOT take photographs!' The hordes of Japanese tourists around me, hearing this, chattered to each other: 'What did that say?'

'I think it said it's OK to take photographs.' Flash, flash, chatter, chatter.)

In contrast, you can't go up close to a Terracotta Warrior: no touch. Mind you, that may be just as well. All manner of rumours surround what may be yet to be discovered in the unexcavated sections: booby-traps of archers on either side, rivers of mercury and so on. Perhaps you get mercury poisoning just by touch? The Chinese seem in no hurry to continue the excavation and find out. They should hire the Wombles to do the job. If there aren't Terracotta Wombles guarding the underground gardens, that is.

There is one modern touch to this old-fashioned exhibition – or it may be an old touch. Peter Kay used to claim that English castles were vulnerable because the invaders could get in through the gift shop. Today, no self-respecting visitor attraction allows you to leave without visiting its shop. While the warriors themselves don't bar your exit at Xi'an, it is impossible to leave without experiencing the full effect of one of those modern cathedrals, the shopping mall. My notes do not record a single memorable fact about it. Unlike the warriors, I have a feeling that the shopping centre will not achieve immortality. As one academic publication puts it: 'If You've Seen One, You've Seen the Mall.'

As we walked out into the hot afternoon sun, taking swigs from our bottles of water, we found one more example of the Womble-ness of Xi'an. People recycle plastic bottles all over China. Helen had noticed the avid collection of empties back at the Summer Palace in Beijing. The recyclers of Xi'an have a more aggressive approach: they come up and demand the bottle before you've finished with it. In the same way that small boys in Istanbul dog your footsteps, suggesting that you visit their brothers' carpet shops, middle-aged Xi'an women in baseball caps walk with you as you brandish your plastic bottle. I suspect they were relatives of the women who tried to escort us along the Great Wall, in the hope that we would buy their books, T-shirts, tattoos, stained glass windows or whatever other merchandise was on offer.

In this case, as we didn't oblige the recyclers by drinking up and handing over the goods, frustration set in. One woman started using a bottle from her existing stock, pushing it with some persistence into Helen's groin. As sales tactics go, this was novel but not a success.

And so ended our brush with Xi'an, in Shaanxi province, from which Shansi Womble got her name (unless it was from Shanxi province next door). The rest of our adventures in China – the sandstorm in Dunhunag, our guide's outrage in Urumqi when we opted to go to the park instead of a carpet factory, being mistaken for a Scottish vicar in Kashgar, driving through the white nightmare nowhere of the Tien Shan mountains to Kyrgyzstan – were still to come.

Shansi is not a major character in the early Wombles books, nor in the original TV series. In *The Wombles Go Round the World*, as four older Wombles go east and west, Shansi and Alderney have to cover their duties in an overstretched burrow. As a result, Shansi works hard – a quality she shares with the people of Xi'an and its province. Perhaps she will get her chance in a future TV adaptation. *Wombles: the Next Generation*, anyone?

One other Womble got his name from a Far Eastern location. Time to travel south and east of China…

BUNGO

The audience stopped shuffling and talking. Her performance was about to begin.

The song struck up, and she danced. Her hair was black, in a topknot, framing pink cheeks and red lips. Bright pink peonies blazed on a black robe with red underlining and a wide white band around the waist. She turned to the left, holding both hands flat in parallel and flicking a pink and white fan open with her right. Every pair of eyes followed her as she turned from side to side, bringing her arms up, down, across, and through the routine again and again.

She raised the fan, open, beside her head, then caressed it from left to right in front of her waist seven times, as if chiding some impertinent insect. The fan came to rest inches from her chest as the music finished. She half-bowed and took the applause.

Throughout the performance, her expression hadn't wavered. But then it couldn't. She was about a foot tall and electronics controlled her. On the second floor of an office block on the north-western coast of Japan, the robot *geisha* was here for our entertainment and education.

A young female presenter, in black corporate T-shirt and trousers, stepped out from behind a podium and spoke in a high, sing-song voice that echoed the music we had just heard. Her explanations remained a mystery – as neither Helen nor I speak Japanese – but the rest of the audience enjoyed the spiel. Couples with small children, three old women in wheelchairs; none of them appeared to fit the Western identikit geek profile. They might have been watching a demonstration of cake-making.

It was just another day, another piece of public relations for Robosquare, a research and education initiative from the city government of Fukuoka, on Japan's southernmost main island, Kyushu. Robosquare described its three goals as:

'Increasing familiarity with robots... Putting robots on display to draw visitors to the facility so visitors can experience robots firsthand and increase their awareness of them.

'Being an educational facility for learning about robots... Fostering the development of future human resources through supporting the study of robotics technology by primary, junior high, and senior high school students.

'Production of robots... Collaborating with robot-related enterprises, networking, and providing support for those enterprises.'

The robot *geisha* – and for that matter the use of store space in a tower block owned by a TV channel and shared with shopping centres and offices – fell into the first category. She had fallen silent as other models took up the charm offensive.

A four-foot-high robot, with a cartoon mouth and dots for eyes on its computer-screen head, and a squat square base in place of legs and feet, held a rack of promotional tissue packs in one artificial claw. The audience queued up to say hello, hear its reply and receive a tissue pack each, in the manner of a Communion wafer.

'No, you cannot buy robots here,' the presenter told me. 'Although, sometimes, the models go into production. Look at this one, for example.'

We examined another four-foot-high model, decked out in white and orange with an oval head in the shape of a modern projector. The presenter pulled one of its ears away from its head on a wire, and spoke into it.

'This model is an intercom, to help you if you are lost. It can project a map of where you need to go, onto a screen. When no visitors are around, it vacuums the floor. One of these is in a major shopping centre, but there are no others.'

The presenter didn't understand my question about the cost of such a robot, or felt the information was of commercial sensitivity. Either way, she avoided answering. No doubt it was expensive – though you wouldn't have to pay wages. It would be of more practical use (though less entertainment value) than a singing Womble.

We had brought the non-singing Bungo with us to Japan and, earlier that morning in a deserted shopping centre, we'd met a modern Japanese equivalent of C3P0, trundling round the fourth floor. It hadn't been doing anything of obvious use, and could be halted by the simple method of standing a few inches in front of it. Still, its eyes lit up and if the electricity supply was on, it could move without human intervention, which was more than could be said for Bungo.

Helen, meanwhile, had gone to the far corner of the store, to see a woman about a dog.

His name was Aibo and his coat was black and glossy. His ears and tail were made from the same material, which looked like brown-grey oversize paperclips. Aibo used to be in production, but these days he moves around his own L-shaped pen in the Robosquare store. A matrix of small lights in his head and across his back glowed red and blue, when someone spoke to him, and when he replied in a voice so high-pitched it was close to inaudible (except for other robot dogs, I assume).

If you leaned close enough to his ears when you spoke, he might obey your commands. The range to which he responded included *osuwari* (sit down), *fusete* (lay down) or *hidari* (turn left). He could also dance. The command for this, in Japanese, is: 'Dance'. That may be overstating the case, as all I saw him do was to cock his right back leg upwards, in a manner that would alarm any lamppost in the area.

Aibo's function was to entertain; Paro had more practical use. Paro was a robot designed to resemble a baby harp seal, right down to the big, soulful eyes. Hospitals and nursing homes in Japan, we were told, were reluctant to use animals in therapy exercises, despite the psychological and physiological effects. Animals, after all, could scratch, bite and pass on infections. Paro had no such off-putting habits. Beneath his soft white artificial fur were seven 'actuators' as well as tactile, auditory, visual and posture sensors. As I stroked him, Paro stirred under my hand and let out gentle, seal-like sounds of contentment.

Paediatric wards, nursing homes and day centres use Paro's brother seals to relax young and elderly patients, and to encourage them to communicate with carers and fellow patients. Analysis of patients' neural patterns has shown improving brain activity levels as a result of use of the robot seals. Robosquare reports one estimate that 84 million people round the world may be suffering from dementia by 2040 and concludes that Paro and his like may become crucial in preventing this condition.

How easy it seemed to be to manipulate people's moods and behaviour, with the help of a cuddly robot seal, I thought, as I continued to stroke Paro.

***

Funny robots, cute robots, useful robots: they're all part of a Japanese love of technology and gadgets. As Helen and I travelled between Honshu, Skikoku and Kyushu islands, we came across this in all manner of places. Steeling ourselves for the walk from Kyoto station to our hotel, we inserted a few hundred yen in a vending machine that discharged rice triangles in soy sauce, or fried chicken.

At one of Fukuoka station's cavernous shopping arcades, this went one step further, in noodle restaurants where you ordered your meal from a vending machine by the front door, handing your ticket to the restaurant staff before going to your table. I thought this was brilliant; no dithering over the menu, no worrying about how long it would take the waiter to bring your change.

Technology asserted itself in the bathroom as well. Anyone who has been to Japan, or read about it, may be familiar with the Mission Control level of buttons, options and instructions which come with the simple act of sitting on a toilet. More often than not, it will be a hot seat, or at least warm. Frankie Howerd used to acknowledge the audience's welcome for his act by saying: 'I do like a warm hand on my entrance.' Frankie would have loved Japanese toilets. The cubicles in some public facilities incorporated a baby-holder, a seat halfway up the wall into which you could place your small infant, securing him or her with a bar across the front while you did what you had to do.

No discussion of technology in Japan would be complete without mentioning the trains. A greater contrast with the dilapidated meandering charm of our Trans-Siberian trip to Tomsk would be hard to imagine. The trains, whether they were intercity bullet or city subway service, arrived at the same position relative to the platform, every time. There was no pausing on the subway while the doors opened, closed, opened again, closed again, opened yet again and closed yet again (if you've been on the London Underground, you'll know what I mean). There were no delays at bullet train stops while passengers bought wares from the platform; in Japan, a purser – a younger version of the British trolley lady of offices of yesteryear – wheeled food and drink along the cars. Her hair was in a bun, and her sensible white blouse and black pinstriped skirt were offset with an apron with diagonal tapering stripes of blue, brown, purple and green and a matching neckerchief. The purser and the ticket inspector, a young man in navy uniform with gold braid and peaked cap, bowed whenever they entered or left the car, as well as when they acknowledged passengers, made a sale, checked a ticket or did anything at all.

Meanwhile, gadgetry continued to do its work. The seats on the first train we boarded, in Osaka, turned 180 degrees at the press of a button, to enable a thorough cleaning operation before departure.

Punctuality, efficiency and service encouraged a sense of pleasant compliance in the passengers. As the train drew up to the platform, they queued, ramrod straight. Once on board, they consulted their mobile phones or read a sports magazine, or a newspaper (to check their shares) or a comic - although on the bullet train, you have to go to the interstices between carriages in order to make phone calls. On the longer journeys, many fell asleep. The bullet trains included one carriage where smoking was allowed but, on the Fukuoka-Hijemi line, I saw four or five people smoking, at most.

Very few passengers bothered with the views, even of the picturesque terraced rice fields. Some pulled down the trays on the back of the seats in front of them, to eat the lunch they had bought in a *bento* box from the station. ('You may not always know what you're eating,' a guidebook had told us. 'But it's sure to be fresh and local.' This was not as reassuring as the writer might have expected.) Older women travelling together as friends might indulge in conversation; businessmen, the majority of the intercity passengers, did not. They were a study in neutrality and conformity, with their charcoal suits, white shirts (some striped), neutral ties, black socks and black shoes.

To warn us of an impending stop, the bilingual electronic displays in each carriage were supplemented with jolly two or three-bar musical jingles and a bilingual public address announcement: 'We will soon make a brief stop at Okayama...' The English version of the message tended to be in an American accent, though there was an Australian lilt to the messages as we approached Kyoto. Some announcements were longer than others. Leaving Osaka, one male monologue in Japanese took so long that Helen speculated: 'He's not talking about the train at all. He's telling us the details of why his wife's left him...'

The musical jingles followed us around Japan, on the city streets as well as on the trains. At traffic lights, when it was safe to walk, the system produced a one-note bird-like chirp or a cuckoo sound. Pedestrians stood stock still if the signs were red – whether traffic was 100 yards or four miles away. When the signs turned green, they came to life like automatons or toys. I'd come across a form of this extreme discipline in Berlin, one cold Christmas, when snow shovelled off the road sat at pedestrian crossings, overwhelming my boots. But Berlin pedestrians may move their head from side to side as they wait, or fidget with their umbrella; their Japanese counterparts did neither.

In Kyoto, as we walked from castles to temples to cafés and back, a strange bing-bong noise followed us. We could never work out whether it emanated from public toilets or subway stations. I kept expecting the female public address announcer from *The Prisoner's* fictional village to say: 'It's going to be a lovely day today!'

On pavements and in parks, yellow lines divided the walkways into two – one lane for cyclists and one for walkers. Fukuoka's main park walkway had a third, for joggers. Cyclists did not seem to honour the divide, but the polite ring-rings of their bells as they came up behind us meant there was no chance of an accident.

All this order, precision, and politeness, even in some of Japan's largest cities, was striking. If Jane Austen had written a novel about Japan, it would have been called *Safety and Sedation.*

On the other hand, maybe I was being harsh on the Japanese, and all this order and obedience was their way of dealing with some of the disasters, natural and manmade, which afflict their country. We had been due to visit Tokyo but, following the recent earthquake, had amended our itinerary to go to Kyoto instead. Now we were on a fast train from Fukuoka to a city that, twice in living memory, had come close to death.

***

'There was a bad smell over Dokai Bay, and nobody knew why.'

The voiceover was matter-of-fact, as if these things happened every day. But then, by the 1960s, things had changed for the city of Kitakyushu and its fishing harbour, as the mini-exhibition in Kitakyushu's Environment Museum was keen to tell us.

Early 20th century industrialisation led to a fall in fish catch levels, and all fishing rights were gone by 1963. In 1957 a man drowned in the bay; the cause was unproven, but alarm spread among the local people. The following year, a survey of the bay's contents found cyanide, cadmium, arsenic and mercury in large quantities. More than 1000 factories operated around the bay – few treated their waste water, and many emptied it into the bay – so the problems were not surprising. Legislation brought a stop to this, imposing tough environmental standards.

Also, dredging of the bay began in the early 1970s at enormous financial cost, of which local companies had to bear over 70%. By 1976 water in the bay met all environmental standards. Since then, over 120 types of fish and crustaceans, along with more than 500 types of aquatic organisms, have returned to the bay. What had been known as Japan's Dead Sea is now thriving with life.

Humans, as well as fish, suffered from the effects of pollution in the area. Another part of the museum's exhibitions told the story of the elementary school at Tobata. Between its opening in 1956 and its closure in 1977, the school was surrounded by more than 80 factories. Eighty tons of soot per square feet fell every month in the region, and the school suffered from more soot than its cleaning machines could handle. Numerous school medical complaints followed, with a strong correlation between absences and higher levels of atmospheric pollution. Parents tried to improve things by planting more than 100 different varieties of foliage in the school grounds – but only willow and oleander came to maturity.

By 1965, local housewives had had enough. They made an 8mm movie 'Desire for blue skies' showing the extent of pollution in Tobata. They would have to spend all day washing as the smoke just made washing dirty all the time. As a test, they put old trays on verandahs; the trays filled with soot. Respiratory organs suffered damage too.

After consulting a university professor about the likely effects on human health, the housewives completed their documentary and gave a copy direct to the mayor. Local antipollution laws, holding local firms fully accountable for what they did, followed. In 1972, 54 Kitakyushu firms made a mutual agreement to switch to low pollution fuel and to take other measures to reduce their corporate impact on the environment.

Kitakyushu is now promoting itself as a model eco-city for others to follow. Much of the rest of its Environment Museum's content – or the presentation, in any case – is aimed at children. On computer screens, cartoon frogs and worms challenged visitors to a series of quiz questions about the daily use of water, electricity and other essentials.

Sliding displays depicted penguins disappearing as a result of global warning. To improve understanding of an excess of CO_2 in the atmosphere, a pinball machine (what else?) was on hand.

Wall charts explained the significance, and life cycles, of ecological commodities and raw materials in daily life, and publicised Kitakyushu's environmental programme and plans. A Reuse Corner displayed a collection of second-hand clothes that were available for exchange – which reminded me of the Orinoco store in Oxfordshire – and signs encouraged visitors to donate unwanted books and CDs.

For all this interaction, information and enthusiasm for all things environmental, the main target audience – children – wasn't there. I exaggerate – one little girl was there, with her father, gazing with fascination at a model eco-house. The two-storey model incorporated solar panels – using flashing lights to indicate their locations – and, to my surprise, a car outside the front door. The man of the house was washing the car (or recharging it, if it was an electric car: the model wasn't clear on this point). At the back of the house, a man lay asleep on a sofa. In the back garden, another man reclined in a deckchair, reading a book. A bespectacled boy frolicked in a small paddling pool with his dog; which one of them would be cleaner for this, I wasn't sure. The only person doing anything active was a girl in dungarees tending the garden.

Museum staff had been coming and going as Helen and I worked our way through the exhibits. I put their bemused smiles down to the fact that we were 30 years older than their typical visitors. But as we were preparing to leave, a tall, studious young man in a blue tracksuit top and white trousers accosted us.

'Have you found the museum interesting? Thank you so much for visiting...'

We assured him we had found the museum interesting.

'Would you like a tour of the Eco-House? It's only next door...'

The full-scale Eco-House was not as interesting as the model in the museum: no electric cars, no flashing lights, no co-bathing humans and dogs. There was plenty of light, clever use of space, an abundance of light wood and a good deal of piping. Something outside looked like a wind turbine.

'The wind turbine is a special type,' explained Kato, our guide. 'It doesn't emit sounds which hurt the human ear, unlike some turbines. It is an experimental model at this stage. There is other experimental work being done near Aso.'

I remarked that we were older than the typical visitor to the museum.

'Yes. We always begin by asking what separates humans from animals...' He paused in expectation for a reply.

'A sense of humour?' I ventured.

'The answer is garbage,' said Kato.

I was taken aback; he had seemed so polite.

'Humans create garbage, animals don't.'

Ah, right. Helen and I nodded.

'Children say the difference is big brains, or technology, but the answer is garbage.'

We went up to the first floor – which in Japan is called the second floor – and perused some promotional leaflets on a table on the landing.

'We have built twenty of these show homes round Japan,' Kato continued. 'But not many people are building eco-houses yet. Materials are expensive at the moment; in time they will be cheaper.'

I asked him how recent disasters in the north-east had affected matters.

'People thought the whole thing was a waste of money before. But the latest disasters have changed some people's minds.'

Kato had no time for the hypocritical conventions (™Great Britain, since goodness knows when) of spending time lamenting the lives lost and the damage done by the earthquake. He was here to promote eco-friendly living and building; if bad news for someone else was good news for Kitakyushu's environmental projects, so be it.

'People from elsewhere in Japan think that Kitakyushu is a dirty city still, but it isn't. We have to learn to divide our energy – using wind, solar and hydrogen.'

Looking out of the window, I saw the hulk of an old blast furnace – the first ever to come to Kitakyushu. But as Kato explained, the traditional enemy of responsible environmental living was now serving its cause.

'Hydrogen comes as a by-product from the local steel works, and we can use that energy. If there is no sun on a particular day, and no wind, we need other energy. Factories are equated with pollution in people's minds. We want to turn that round and show they can work for good.'

As I considered this challenge, Kato asked the questions I'd been dreading:

'So why are you so interested in this project? Why did you come to Japan?'

As I sighed and unzipped my backpack, Helen rolled her eyes. We'd introduced Bungo to several Japanese on the journey. His appearance tended to produce smiles and giggles, the loudest from two respectable middle-aged ladies having their respectable middle-aged lunch next to us in the lake café in Fukuoka. Explanations of Bungo's origins, purpose and influence on our travels were more difficult.

This time was different. Kato spoke fluent English, understood it and was the first Japanese whose eyes didn't glaze over as I explained Bungo's Womble origins and significance as an early symbol of recycling. Like other Japanese, he smiled when he saw Bungo; it was the first time we had seen him smile.

'Aha! Perhaps Bungo can come back to Japan and teach our children about the Wombles!'

To forestall negotiations of Bungo's teaching consultancy – rent-free burrow, daily picnics, that sort of thing – Helen took photos of Kato holding Bungo, and giving him a short lecture on the benefits of eco-housing. Like many people we met in Japan, Kato was not camera-shy. We promised to email the pictures to him.

'Come back soon,' he said as we left the house and waved goodbye.

As we walked back towards the railway station for our return trip to Fukuoka, one mystery remained. Where were all the children?

'That'll be the space shuttle, then,' said Helen.

'*What?*'

'That'll be the space shuttle. *Discovery*, I think.'

I followed her gaze. Yes, there was a space shuttle on our right... close to Kitakyushu's version of the London Eye. There were hordes of schoolchildren, sitting on the pavement as their teachers negotiated their entrance into the Space World theme park. No wonder they weren't in the museum. They were too excited about seeing the Venus Grand Prix, or taking part in a Black Hole Scramble, or going on a Mission to Mars. The museum might come later, after they'd had a chance to spend some of their ten-year-olds' energy.

In the warmth of the afternoon sun, I stood in the middle of a Kitakyushu triangle: blast furnace, theme park, eco-house and museum; past, present and – if Kato had his way and the Eco-House became a nationwide success – future. At least the city would have a future of some sort, after choking itself close to death. But Kitakyushu might have died even before then, if it hadn't been for some cloudy weather.

***

'My parents were Hiroshima survivors.'

Mrs Tanaka nodded as she spoke, in that peculiar fashion that some people do, which reminds me without fail of donkeys and mechanical pumpheads and Mike Brearley's batting technique. But, beyond confirming that she was a lifelong Hiroshima resident and a member of the Peace Volunteer Corps, she did not elaborate on this statement. Mrs Tanaka was our Goodwill Guide in Hiroshima. Goodwill Guides are local residents who show you round their Japanese town or city, for no charge other than their food, travel and admission ticket expenses. I'd emailed her in advance to ask if she would take us round the Peace Park. She had replied: 'I would like to recommend Miyajima' – an island in Japan's Inland Sea, in the north-west part of Hiroshima Bay. If we had already visited Miyajima, then she would take us to the Peace Park.

So, before we met Mrs Tanaka, Helen and I had visited Hiroshima's Peace Park and its Memorial Museum. After its early days as a 'city of schools and shopping districts', Hiroshima became more industrialised – and more militarised – as the city entered the twentieth century. The most effective items on display were a pair of circular models under glass. One model showed the city before the US Air Forces dropped an atomic bomb on the morning of 6 August 1945; the other showed the city just afterwards, with 70% of the buildings destroyed.

As we examined the artefacts of charred clothing, the waxwork reconstructions of people whose bodies had melted in the attack and the information boards about the subsequent effects of radiation on residents and their descendants, we could appreciate the narrow escape from a similar fate of Kitakyushu, or Kokura as it was known then. Kokura was to be the target for the second atomic bomb, but – so the story goes – three attempts to drop it failed, due to clouds and smoke from nearby Yahata. That second bomb was dropped on Nagasaki.

The museum's text boards adopted a careful, neutral tone towards the events leading up to 1945, to the extent of failing to give reasons for some of the key background decisions (such as Japan's invasion of Manchuria). Any passion or moral outrage was reserved for the upper floors of the exhibition, which catalogued Hiroshima's post-war role in campaigning for the abolition of nuclear weapons. We could only hope that the many Japanese schoolchildren in the Peace Park that day – girls in sailor suit uniforms, boys in high-collared black jackets – would be as lucky as our generation, and would never have to fight or die in a war.

The next day, we met Mrs Tanaka for our journey by train and ferry to Miyajima. Mrs Tanaka was about four foot tall, dark haired with a centre parting, and she wore a blue kimono with floral patterns, and white socks with two toes to accommodate her wooden sandals. She carried a light blue umbrella for shade and her notes and other items in a green Harrods bag with a Scottie dog on the side.

'Ah, yes, my daughter gave me the bag as a gift when she visited to London. I have been to London too – and Edinburgh! And I studied English Language and economic history and the French Revolution. At Oxford Brookes University. Very good university.'

On the ferry to Miyajima, we got a look at its famous Shinto *torii* gate on the way. *Torii* gates act as a spiritual barrier, protecting those within from the outside world. The gate, Mrs Tanaka assured us, was one of Japan's Top Three sites of Scenic Beauty. One thing about it was puzzling me. Why was it orange when all the postcards and photos I had seen showed it as red?

'Ah,' nodded Mrs Tanaka. 'The orange paint is – how you say it? – more friendly to the environment.'

As the ferry ploughed on, we were treated to a selection of Mrs Tanaka's wedding photos, taken in 1971. The bride and groom were drinking *sake*.

'Yes, *sake* has a spiritual significance,' she explained. 'My daughter will not be drinking it yet. She does not have a boyfriend!'

More nodding.

We disembarked from the ferry. As we walked along the edge of the island, I asked Mrs Tanaka about the legend that it was forbidden for anyone to be born or die on the island, due to its sacred Shinto status.

'Oh, yes, that is true. There was no cemetery or hospital. Now there is a small hospital, but it does not have a maternity unit.'

The Shinto religion was, among other things, good for the local deer. Local people believed them to be messengers of the gods and, as a result, would not kill them. This non-practice continues today. All over Miyajima, deer wandered around loose, unconcerned by humans. One of them stuck its head onto the counter of a photography kiosk as if expecting service. Others harassed a couple and their pram-bound child by trying to drink its milk.

Miyajima boasts a number of shrines, of which the most famous is Itsukushima, a UNESCO World Heritage Site. Many shrines had a purification room opposite, in which believers would wash their hands to purify themselves before prayer. The believer then approaches the shrine, bows their head, claps their hands twice to get their god's attention and prays.

One section of Itsukushima was devoted to little wooden hanging mini-plaques with prayers, some from students with messages praying for success into getting into university. The reverse of each mini-plaque had a standard picture with a white rabbit, as it was the Chinese year of the rabbit. One message, in English, was from a married woman praying for the health of her sick brother. Another wished for good luck for the local baseball team, Hiroshima Carp, a name that was one transposition of letters away from a gift for reporters if and when they lost.

(Japan seems to like teetering on the edge of unfortunate Anglicisations, as I reflected in Fukuoka when visiting the department store ASSE.)

We passed more *torii* gates, smaller versions of the red/orange version in the harbour. These gates were covered in little pieces of paper.

'The paper reinforces the *torii's* physical barrier against intruders, and protection of those who are inside,' said Mrs Tanaka. I reflected that modern secular Britain is prone to using paper as a barrier, but in conjunction with bureaucrats rather than gates.

Towards the entrance of the Itsukushima shrine, we bumped into the back of a procession that would be familiar, whatever the religion: a wedding. The bride wore a white kimono with an elaborate hood-over-head arrangement, reminiscent of Grace Jones in her mad, Russell Harty-hitting phase. Otherwise, the dress code was strict.

'Unmarried women have colourful kimonos, married women wear black kimonos,' was Mrs Tanaka's succinct explanation. The married women, I noticed, could express their individuality through wearing quite elaborate designs of black. All the men were in dark Western-style suits.

The other principal temple we visited was the Daisho-in Buddhist complex. The Daisho-in is one of the most prestigious temples in western Japan. Access is via a flight of stairs, with *sutras* – short aphorisms - on brass cylinders attached to the balustrade, so that believers could spin them as they climb.

We tried the free herb tea, which contained no less than 16 herbs for good health, at the Worshippers' Hall. On 8 March each year, we learned, there is a ceremony at the temple to give thanks to old kitchen knives that are no longer usable. I wondered why they didn't try to reuse them in some other form.

The temple area contained many statues, some of them twee or in dubious taste. A few depicted *tanuki*, the Japanese raccoon dog which looks like a cross between a badger and a raccoon. *Tanuki* are good luck symbols in Japan; they are celebrated as mischievous creatures and believed to be capable of changing their shape at will. Well, if *you* looked like a cross between a badger and a raccoon, you might think that was a handy thing to be able to do.

Inside the various temples and shrines within Daisho-in were offerings of fruit, either fresh oranges and apples or tinned peaches and mandarin oranges. Alan Bennett said that 'Life is rather like a tin of sardines: we are all of us looking for the key.' The question for Buddhists in Japan may be whether life has a tin-opener. If there isn't, they may not be able to enjoy (tinned) peach on earth.

***

Food – Japanese food – has been a magnet for the interest of philosophers over the years. In his book of Japanese snapshots *Atomic Sushi*, Simon May writes: 'When I was unexpectedly invited to be a visiting professor of philosophy at Tokyo University... my first thought was: "the sushi!" – a year of unlimited access to those glistening strips of the world's freshest fish draped over beguilingly tepid, gently vinegary, sticky rice...'

And before Simon May, there was Roland Barthes. Long before he visited Japan, Barthes was writing what he described as 'ideological critique[s] of the language of mass culture', deconstructing everyday objects to rescue their significance from contemporary 'mythologies'. He was comparing new cars to 'Christ's robe [or] the airships of science-fiction' because of the central role of plastic, with its quasi-magical suggestions of perfection... 'one keenly feels the edges of the windows, one feels along the wide rubber grooves which link the back window to its metal surround.'

The old Citroen-groper found his perfect subject for analysis in Japan and the Japanese. Barthes contrasted Western-style violent 'cutting and piercing' of foodstuffs using knives and forks with the use of chopsticks, which ensure that 'the foodstuff never undergoes a pressure greater than is precisely necessary to raise and carry it'. Japanese meals, like Japanese cities, did not have the traditional centre that Western minds expected, but were 'a collection of fragments'.

Given his keen interests in plastic and food, it's a mystery why Barthes didn't write about the most distinctive feature of many Japanese restaurants: the plastic replicas of dishes which sit in the window, or on a table outside, and which are a great help to diners like me who can't read Japanese. Point, choose: simple. You can see what Barthes meant about plastic perfection. Most of the replicas tilt towards you without, of course, the soup or sauce threatening to escape onto your clean white shirt.

On consideration, maybe Barthes didn't write about the replica dishes because their simple combination of elegance and function was self-explanatory. As someone else wrote, sometimes a plastic replica Japanese menu item is just a plastic replica Japanese menu item.

Thoughts of philosophers were buzzing around my head because we were about to go on 'The Philosopher's Walk' – a mile-long walk through part of Kyoto where Nishida Kataro, a philosopher and professor at the city's university, had been in the habit of taking his morning constitutional. The standard route is to go from north to south, from the Ginkakuji Temple with its Silver Pavilion to the Nanzen-ji Temple, a head temple of a Zen sect. However, in the words of Kierkegaard, 'life can only be understood backwards; but it must be lived forwards.' So we opted to start at the end, with Zen – after a visit to the nearby city zoo.

Names and titles have more significance than we might suppose. My thoughts would have been different – or less – if the route had been known as 'The Tourist's Walk', or 'The Bricklayer's Walk', or 'The Angler's Walk'. Calling it 'The Philosopher's Walk' puts the pressure on you to be thoughtful, and philosophical, and contemplative. It's not fair, I'm telling you. (Thank goodness I don't have the qualifications to have to be professorial on top of all that.)

So, there we were, walking a gentle uphill gradient by a canal lined with cherry trees, on a cloudy afternoon. We'd arrived in Japan a few weeks after the cherry blossom season, and most of the tourists had disappeared along with most of the blossom. The only other life we encountered on the first part of the walk was a white cat lounging on a bench, staring with covetous hunger at the large orange-and-white carp in the canal. I couldn't identify the type of cat. If it had been fluffier, with madder eyes, I'd have had no problem recognising it as a Blofeld's cat, the sort whose human companions live in secret bases underneath volcanoes. As its type was uncertain, I decided it must be a Schrödinger's cat.

In between the various rail, bus, tram, ferry and taxi journeys, we'd managed to fit in a walk or two. In Matsuyama we had walked the 'Road of the Haiku', and had stopped every so often to look at the rocks and boulders which bore examples of this famous Japanese form of three-line poetry. Unlike the signage in hotels, railway stations and other public places there and elsewhere on our trip, the Matsuyamans did not choose to translate their public haiku into English. But there was no point in moaning: we would just have to write our own (in English). So, as we trudged from temple to temple searching for a teashop which was open, I did so, obeying the conventions of a mention of the seasons and a 5-7-5 syllable count across the lines:

Springtime in Japan
Walking with our backpacks on
Uphill is harder

I felt I had used our specific situation to sum up a universal truth, in traditional Japanese poetic form.

'What's the Japanese for "*Don't call us, we'll call you*?"' Helen wondered.

The clouds were beginning to open and the rain was threatening to spoil the walk and its contemplative calm. After all, as a philosopher said: 'A man cannot empty his mind if his shoes are filling with water.' (All right, I made that one up. Going on Philosopher's Walks does that to you.)

The lights of a café came into view on our right. In this case, the menu options were represented by colour clipart. The caption to one option in particular caught our eye:

'*Warabimochi* and *matcha*'

Matcha, we knew, was one Japanese variant on green tea: the bubbling kind which comes in a bowl and makes you wonder if eye of newt has been tossed in for flavour. What was *warabimochi*? The English translation was given as 'Bracken jelly with soy flour'.

Helen and I looked at each other. From the warmth of my backpack, Bungo looked at us, then at the menu again. Of all the Zen joints in all the towns, in all the world, we'd walked into this one: a café serving Womble food.

The elderly female owner bustled us in with a wave of her bent arm and the words: 'English menu, come in.'

We didn't need the encouragement; we were in, out of the rain, on comfortable seats in a quiet café. And, minutes later, the food arrived.

The colour clipart had not been as precise as plastic food replicas, so we weren't sure what to expect. For whatever reason, I wasn't expecting bracken jelly to be… green. The dusting of soy flour, along with the greenness, gave the ensemble an unearthly quality.

Bungo tries some bracken jelly in Kyoto

Being braver than me, Helen was first to try it. Being greedier, Bungo tried to get there second. The owner, who had come back to retrieve the menus, was nonplussed. I went through the explanation routine, without obvious success.

How did it taste, you ask? Like jelly... not as sweet as some Japanese sweet dishes, but (thank goodness) nowhere near as bitter as, say, a pickled plum. Having a sweet tooth, I might have preferred the deep fried Mars bars from Inverbeg.

All that remained was to pay the bill, complete the walk and admire Ginkakuji's gravel garden, raked with infinite care and precision – no hint of rubbish here – and to reflect on another successful day for Bungo. He had seen Womble food, a few days after we had tracked down his very own bridge.

***

Of all the places we'd visited after which Wombles got their names, Bungo represented the biggest challenge. Its main usage was for a province in north-eastern Kyushu, between the 7th and 16th centuries. It had been the product of a splitting of Toyo province; Bungo was one half, its literal meaning 'the back of Toyo'. Bungo province had long since disappeared; the nearest modern equivalent was Oita prefecture.

The name survived in a few places, depending on which map we used. On some, a body of water between Skikoku and Kyushu was identified as Bungo-suido (Bungo Strait). Other maps gave a different name, Hayasui-seto (Hoyo Strait). Still others showed both names, one in the north of the strait and one in the south; and yet others gave one name, Hoyo Strait. As we took the ferry from Yawatahama on Skikoku to Beppu on Kyushu, we waved in all directions, in the hope that the Bungo Strait was somewhere around us. Did travellers in earlier times have the same problem?

'Here Be Dragons.'
'Here Be Dragons and Mammoths.'
'Here Be Mammoths. Definitely No Dragons.'
'Here Be... Nothing Much. Nothing to See, Move Along.'
'Your Guess is as Good as Ours.'

We found out, too late, that we had passed by Bungo Takeda – or Bungo Takada as some maps render it, north of Beppu in the north-eastern tip of Kyushu. The ruins of the keep of a 12th century castle give an excellent view of the Aso mountains, but we missed it.

So, as we strolled towards Kokura Castle in Kitakyushu, it looked as if we would have to settle for having travelled through the area which used to be Bungo province, and going by ferry across, or close to, the Bungo Channel.

The information board outside Kokura Castle stated that it was built in 1602 by Tadaoki Hosokawa, who had been given 'the Buzen area and two districts of Bungo as his fief.' That cheered us up. The exhibitions and displays inside were entertaining. One glass case – caption in Japanese, not English - contained copies of a stick, a carrot and a fish. It must have been an early example of Japanese management methods, with the fish available for appropriate slapping across workers' faces.

An animated film gave a brief glimpse into the lives of people in Kokura in the 17th century, through the eyes of time-travelling raccoons who had angered the god of the castle by trying to squat in his temple, and were sent back to learn about the castle's past. As a historian I objected to the underlying idea that history is something you have to study as a punishment, but the raccoons were a novel way of conveying the information.

We left the castle and stopped to study a map in order to find our way back to the station. For some reason, the number of bridges over the Onga River caught Helen's attention.

'Look at these bridge names…'

'Any reason?'

'Just *look*!'

I looked. A sequence of bridges seemed to have a Japanese name, and a themed designation:

Muromachi – bridge of fire
Tokiwa – bridge of wood
Katsuyami – bridge of stone
Ogai – bridge of seagulls
Nakano – bridge of the sun
Murasakigawa – bridge of iron
Nakashima – bridge of wind
And the final one:
Bungo – bridge of sound

If any residents of Kitakyushu read this, and saw a couple of *gaijin* walking along the river that day carrying backpacks and a small stuffed toy, you now know what we were doing. I hope you didn't stall your car, crash your bike or walk into a lamppost or anything else.

The themes of the bridges helped us to confirm we were going in the right direction. Nakashima sported a tall and splendid windmill sculpture. As its green sails whirled in a cloudless blue afternoon sky, in concert with crows and hawks, we found Bungo Bridge. Signs at either end in Japanese and English confirmed it, and Bungo posed for the appropriate photos, in triumph.

***

As Bungo sat in a spare seat on the flight home, declining the cabin crew's offer of a complimentary drink and cheese roll, it was time to reflect on the trip.

Japan had good claims to being the most Womble-like place we had visited. In addition to the people and places I have described, the parts of Japan we saw were, on the whole, exceedingly tidy. In Kyoto, a middle-aged lady with the lead of her pet poodle in one hand was using a pair of outsize tongs with the other hand to pick up items of rubbish from the gutter as she walked past us.

Evidence of awareness of environmental issues, and enthusiasm for action, was not confined to the staff of the Environmental Museum at Kitakyushu. At the edge of the beach in Fukuoka sat three wind turbines which – so the publicity claimed – could recharge your mobile phone. We found the beach house in which the recharging equipment sat; we couldn't test it because our mobile phones were not compatible.

While in Kyoto, we visited a museum devoted to *manga*, the Japanese comic and cartoon book art which has grown in worldwide popularity, along with its cousin *anime* (Japanese animation). A special exhibition at the time of our visit introduced us to *The Rose of Versailles*, a *manga* set in the French Revolution, depicting historical people such as Marie Antoinette and fictional ones like Oscar, a cross-dressing soldier. *The Rose of Versailles* was much more than a *manga*: it became an animated TV series, then a live action film… does that sound familiar? It also became a stage show and is still performed. While the Wombles came to 1970s TV via a form of stop animation rather than *anime*, a Womble-themed *manga* would be worth seeing.

However, while Japan might have Womble-like qualities, the people didn't remind me of bossy Bungo – quite the opposite. The flipside of all that efficiency and service and organisation and willingness to please was, it seemed to me, a certain quietness, compliance and conformity. No doubt the anarchic, rebellious, subversive side of Japan exists – not, though, in the parts of Japan, including the former Bungo province, which we so enjoyed visiting.

The quest was complete. Except…

ALDERNEY

Except…Alderney.

This younger Womble underwent a transformation, between the original books and the 1990s TV revival. The 1990s Alderney spends much of her time helping Madame Cholet. She lives in a tree rather than in the burrow, looks after the lake rather than the common and flies the Womcopter. Alderney has yellow pigtails and wears a striped shirt and a seashell necklace.

Alderney shares her name with the Channel Island to which Elisabeth Beresford moved. One short plane trip might enable me to meet the creator of the Wombles. The opportunity was too good to miss.

***

'Have you seen the plane?' asked the man queuing at the check-in desk.

I affected nonchalance. 'No. Is it long and thin with bits sticking out of the side?'

He laughed.

'You might want to go to the toilet before you board.'

I had spent a lifetime failing to notice the type of plane on which I was flying, and saw no reason to change now. No doubt my predecessor in the queue – a tall burly Australian in his thirties with a pudding bowl haircut – was winding me up.

By the time the check-in desk opened, the queue had swelled to a dozen people. I looked at my boarding pass: 3F. A window seat – that was good. Mind you, if there were only a dozen passengers, everybody should be able to sit where they liked.

Perhaps the cabin crew would outnumber the passengers. It reminded me of a story about Orson Welles touring midtown America with a one-man show. One performance, to an audience of four, began: 'Good evening. My name is Orson Welles. I'm a writer. I'm an actor. I'm a director. I'm a producer. I'm a businessman. What a shame there's so many of me and so few of you.'

The departures lounge was about twice the size of my lounge, and the calmest departures area I'd ever seen. No small infants were crying, running up and down, getting locked in the toilets or emptying the bins out onto the floor (I have suffered many children at airports who have performed one or more of these acts, and one or two who managed them all).

Men in dark suits waited for their flights to Jersey. I stood next to two of them, who were wearing black ties, too. The lounge was so quiet that every word of their conversation was audible. To my surprise, it was not about takeovers, mergers, acquisitions and credit crunches, but football. I looked closer. One of the men was Harry Redknapp, manager of the Spurs football team – the team I have supported all my life. He had managed Bournemouth, Southampton and Portsmouth in years gone by and still lived on the south coast. Against every football stereotype ever created, he was taller than he seemed on the TV; and more articulate, too. I didn't hear one word about 'the end of the day' or 'the boys done well'. He and his companion were travelling on a budget airline: another cliché shattered. I thought all top-level football players and managers took their own private jets. Harry had gone before I had plucked up the courage to say a word to him, or to get him to autograph my passport.

Now it was time for the Alderney Dozen to board. While waiting, we watched the airline safety demonstration video on a plasma screen by the gate. This was, to my mind, a sensible use of time, and avoided having to put one of the cabin crew through the ritual humiliation of pulling toggles, pointing like the *Wizard of Oz* scarecrow and so on. The video seemed to have been filmed in someone's car; the space in which the actor demonstrated was tiny. The boarding crew, I noticed around this time, were the same people as the check-in crew.

We went through the gate onto the tarmac. A large bus stood before us, ready to perform the traditional task of taking passengers halfway round the airport to justify the driver's job. But we didn't get on. Instead, the boarding crew took us a few yards to the plane.

'Please can we have seats 2A and 2F to board,' said the cheerful slim young man in the fluorescent jacket. 'Thank you... and now 3A and 3F... thank you... and now...'

It was the smallest passenger plane I have ever seen, with just enough room for the company logo on the body and a painting of a puffin on the yellow tail. Everyone's ticket was either A or F. Everyone had a window seat. Each row had two seats; there were seven rows. There were no aisle seats because there was no aisle. There were no toilets.

At last the truth dawned: now I realised why the safety video filming looked so cramped and why there were so few airline staff. This wasn't a plane with plenty of empty spaces, as I'd thought; it was a tiny, full plane.

By standing on glorified packing crates, we boarded two at a time – just like the Ark. The only spare seat was at the front, on the right of the captain, a large man with a mop of grey hair and a luxuriant double chin. My neighbour strapped himself in, slumped over his laptop and dozed off.

'Good morning, everyone,' said double-chin in a calm, clipped tone. 'My name is William and I'm your captain for this morning's flight. Just before we start, I can confirm there are no refreshments, haha!'

The plane was so small we could hear everything. My neighbour showed no sign of waking up. There was a little conversation behind me, but not for long. Soon we climbed over the Channel into a blue sky. The drone of the plane and the monotony of the view – clear sky, calm sea - lulled me into sleep.

I woke with a start to see Alderney looming below us. Double-chin landed the plane with delicacy, as if he was tucking his children into bed, and held my backpack as I got out and took photos of the plane. I collected my luggage from the arrivals area – a shed. I walked out of the airport, to the end of the road and turned right. After ten minutes' stroll along an empty road, I entered St Anne, the capital: two minutes later, I'd found the guesthouse which was my base for the trip.

The sun was blazing down and it felt as if something had been missing from my outward journey. Oh, yes, that was it: stress. There had been no stress at all. Retired pilots used to talk about decades gone by, 'when flying was fun'. Perhaps this was what they'd meant.

***

'DID YOU USE THE EARPLUGS?'

'NO, I FORGOT TO BRING THEM!'

'WHO WAS YOUR PILOT? WILLIAM? WAS HE READING THE PAPER? THEY DO THAT SOMETIMES. ONCE THEY'RE UP IN THE AIR, SOMEONE'S TRACKING THEM, SO THERE ISN'T A LOT TO DO...'

Charles and I had to shout above the sound of the waves to make ourselves heard, as we left the harbour. I'd got in touch with Charles through a mutual contact. He had cancelled a flying lesson that day in order to show me some of the sights of Alderney.

Charles had his own rigid inflatable boat (RIB). The seats looked and felt like the vaulting horses from a gym. The twin engines were at the back. By the wheel was the boat equivalent of a sat-nav, but without a voice. This was a pity, I thought. The bossy female voice in most cars' sat-navs is annoying, but a naval sat-nav with (say) a pirate voice and handy phrases such as 'shiver me timbers' and 'land ahoy' could sell millions.

Charles steered past the edge of the breakwater, into the open water beyond the harbour. I perched on my seat, legs astride, as the boat began to bounce like a bucking bronco.

'Anything which falls in the water here tends to stay there,' Charles had warned me, so every pocket of my waterproofs and backpack was zipped shut.

Charles first came to Alderney in the 1960s, as a schoolboy, then returned several times to meet a friend with a mutual interest in ham radio. He finally moved to the island four years ago from the Surrey-Sussex border 'to get away from it all and have some fun'. Charles was a short, neat man with a wiry body and a greying beard, whose fun came in understated style.

No other boats were in sight as Charles steered round some rocks and the odd collection of weeds in the water. I looked back at the coastline, and the remains of some of the forts built in the 1850s and 1860s as defences against a possible French invasion, and the anti-tank walls, and artillery battery the Germans built when they occupied Alderney during World War II. Then white specks started to appear in the sky, coming closer and closer.

'They're gannets,' Charles explained. 'There are thousands of pairs on Les Etacs.' He pointed to the larger of two rocks just off Alderney's south-west tip.

'You can't hear them because the wind's in the wrong direction. You can't smell them either, for the same reason.'

I was happy to sacrifice the chance to hear the gannets' cries, in return for being saved from their smell. There are several thousands of them, so it might be overpowering.

'Sorry you didn't get to see the puffins,' said Charles. 'They all disappear by the end of July.'

We returned to harbour and to a lunch of crab fishcakes and steak and onion pie. Having avoided the gannets, we now walked into clouds of cigarette smoke. Unlike mainland Britain, smoking in some public places on Alderney was still legal. A recent proposal to ban smoking in public places was the subject of heated debate. The owner of the restaurant where I'd eaten the previous evening had given me copies of two local newsletters, the *Journal* and the *Press*, in which the controversy was raging.

'The *Journal's* been going for years, but someone got annoyed when they started to print it in Guernsey instead of Alderney. So they started up the *Press* to poke them in the eye!' she told me.

Despite their origins in a local spat, the two publications covered many of the same issues. Perhaps that was inevitable on an island which is only three miles long by one and a half miles wide: there is only so much to write about. Both newsletters included impassioned letters arguing for the retention of smoking.

'Stop smoking in bars and at least some will close… staff will be laid off, and rent and tax incomes will fall… why change for a selfish minority?'

'Smoking is about freedom of choice… Alderney has been an attractive place because it has been relatively free from the influence of the "Muesli & Sandals Brigade" who would have us all regulated according to little understood and often unread "reports" purporting to be serious scientific studies…'

'Alcohol may also be on the unhealthy list but are we soon to be told that we are to be deprived of this for health reasons?… Alderney seems to be fast becoming a nanny state…'

I showed the letters to Charles.

'They're idiots,' was his view. 'But then, I'm not a "local".'

So what was he?

'I'm a resident. You have to live here a long time to be considered a "local". There are plenty of second homers, like my neighbours who are only here six months of the year. They're not "locals", either. When you take into account people like the schoolchildren who can only get their A Levels and degrees on the mainland, the real permanent population is nearer 1500 than 2400. But for children's health, if for no other reason, I'd ban smoking in public like a shot if it was up to me.'

Why was he so vehement about it? Charles gave a rueful smile.

'I'm an ex-smoker – 30 a day – so I'm now fervently anti-smoking. Converts are always the loudest preachers...'

After a smoke-free cup of tea at Charles's house, we set out for a walk round the northwest coast. Some of the paths were steep, but plentiful shrubbery on either side would, Charles assured me, prevent anyone falling very far.

'You'd have to be drunk or very unlucky to fall off Alderney,' he said. I thought of Bulgaria and shuddered. Charles was right. We didn't get too close to any cliff edges, and it turned into a glorious, gentle amble past the occasional goat or fellow walker. The walk took us to a view of Fort Tourgis, which the British government built in 1855 as protection for the nearby Breakwater and harbour. The land had been bought recently, said Charles, by a Dutch firm of architects who wanted to turn it into a hotel and conference centre. He was not impressed.

'One of my friends is a priest and he reckons it could make a good place for a spiritual retreat.'

I speculated that the combination of fresh air, good light and remoteness from anywhere might make it attractive for artists.

'Mmm, could do,' said Charles, polite but unconvinced.

We walked for a while and stopped again, this time at an old German bunker.

'This is the local disco,' said Charles.

Was this military code of some sort?

'No, honestly, it's a disco,' he continued. 'There isn't much for the teenagers to do, so they've been encouraged to use this as a base for parties. It gives them a bit of privacy and the rest of the island a bit of peace and quiet.'

Earlier in the week I had gone to the Arts Centre in Victoria Street, St Anne's main road, for a screening of a new American film *The Hangover* ('sponsored by Sam Chadwick's meat draw and bonus ball'). The cinema was run and manned by volunteers. The American lady in the box office assured me that 'you can sit anywhere you want'. She wasn't joking. The 100-seater cinema was three-quarters empty. Her accomplice, a man of about 80 with white hair, a goatee beard, a striped shirt, fawn trousers and a cravat, shuffled around, selling sweets.

Beatles tracks were playing as we waited for the film to start. It did not seem like a cool place for teenagers, who put their feet up on the seats next to me.

An hour into the film came the intermission. Every film at the Alderney Arts Centre gets an intermission, so that the reels can be changed. For those of drinking age, this is not a problem; they go to the Georgian House pub over the road. For young teenagers, there's nothing to do except buy some fruit pastilles, flirt in desultory fashion and wait for part two. So maybe a bunker disco works for them.

Alderney has a reputation as a magnet for those who want to slow down in life, often to retire. Well-known émigrés to the island have included TH White and John Arlott. One unfortunate side effect is that a large proportion of the island population is elderly. In addition to the smoking ban controversy, islanders had been up in arms about the decision to award a £2.5 million contract to build a new residential care home to a Guernsey firm. Their tender came in cheaper and in 33% less time than Alderney firms.

'I reckon the local firms shoot themselves in the foot,' said Charles, as we walked on. 'They drag out the work they do, so it lasts longer. If you're going to tender for work and someone comes in cheaper and quicker than local firms, of course they're going to get the contract. But you won't get any thanks for pointing that out round here.'

The political structures add to a frequent sense of injustice on Alderney. The island has its own legislature known as the States, and sends representatives to Guernsey's equivalent. Taxes, on the other hand, are collected and administered by the Bailiwick of Guernsey, which provides many government functions and some legal jurisdiction in criminal matters. Guernsey also ratifies decisions on the placing of major contracts on Alderney.

I was beginning to get a picture of Alderney and its people. If the Channel Islands were a family, Alderney would be the neglected middle sibling: not old enough to inherit, not large enough to look after itself, not young or small enough to get all the attention, thinks it's unloved, liable to be picked on or get into arguments.

It didn't help that – according to the local newsletters – some islanders believed that their elected representatives were stifling their views. At a recent 'people's meeting', according to the *Journal*, one representative had refused to discuss the care home contract, despite repeated questions from the floor. A cartoon next to the report depicted a speaker saying: 'Now you are all sitting comfortably, we can begin!' The audience had their hands tied to the chairs and were blindfolded.

While we had been discussing this, Charles and I had wandered up to a couple of unimportant looking posts. Charles stopped and looked at me in meaningful fashion.

'Ah, yes,' he said. 'This is Camp Sylt.'

We had come to the dark hole at the heart of Alderney's history.

***

The fate of the Channel Islands in World War II – their occupation by the Germans – is of course well-known. Alderney's experience differed from the other islands in several ways. The British government arranged for the evacuation of everyone on Alderney. Residents had to choose which of their possessions to pack into the one suitcase which they were each allowed to take with them. Most of them ended up in London or Glasgow for the rest of the war.

Nine days after they left, the Germans arrived. They brought slave labour – Russians and Eastern Europeans for the most part – to work on building bunkers, air raid shelters and fortifications. There were three forced labour camps; Lager Sylt was a concentration camp. Estimates of deaths vary between 400 and 700, from a total population of about 6,000. The German commanding officer burned down the camps and destroyed all records relating to their use, shortly before the British liberated Alderney on 16 May 1945.

Islanders weren't able to return until that December. Some of their homes had been stripped of every last piece of wood, as the Germans' need for fuel became more desperate. Other items had been 'rescued' by other islanders or by the French, in the nine days between the evacuation and the occupation. Some of these items never returned; others turned up in other houses on Alderney, prompting many bitter accusations. The island was so short of the basics of 1940s life that the British government had to issue emergency supplies.

The Germans' destruction of the evidence, and the inevitable local reluctance to discuss the occupation, make it a curious experience to stand by the two posts which mark Lager Sylt.

Charles and I read the inscription placed on one post as recently as 2008; neither of us said a word.

During my stay on Alderney, I bumped into one elderly couple on five occasions. Baz and Doris had retired to Guernsey: Baz used to work for Securicor and deliver to Alderney, and he didn't want to fly anywhere far for his holidays, so Alderney was the perfect place. Their sunny dispositions only clouded over once, when Doris talked about her father.

'He had to work in one of the camps here, you know,' she said in a voice with a south-western lilt. 'It was a disgrace, the way the Germans treated him. He came back looking like a skeleton.'

The day after my walk with Charles, I sat in the Issue Room in the Alderney Museum, looking at artefacts from the occupation such as the Red Cross aid parcels dropped into Alderney in 1944, after intense negotiations; and copies of the notice to islanders instructing them to prepare for evacuation in 1940.

I tried to imagine what it must feel like to look back from a boat at your home, and to ask yourself if you will ever see home again. I thought of Doris's father and how anyone could work as a prisoner in a camp where one word out of place could kill you and your family. Not for the first time, I reflected on my own generation and how spoiled, self-indulgent, and lucky we are.

***

The museum itself relied – like the Arts Centre, the tourist information centre and several other activities on this small island – on the efforts of volunteers. As you would expect, there was information on the geology and history of Alderney; there were examples of Stone Age pottery and Bronze Age tools. One room focused on an unnamed

Elizabethan ship wrecked off Alderney in 1575, and a chart detailed – with a little too much glee, I reckoned – seventeen further wrecks between 1901-85 alone. But, of all the museums I have visited, none has housed a section so bursting with pride and passion as this museum's displays about the Alderney Cow.

You may find it hard to believe that such an amiable creature could be the object of such contention, but it is. The museum – which is not large – devotes four wall panels worth of words and images to the controversy.

The first panel asks 'What is the Alderney Cow?' and berates various parties, including Anthony Trollope and *The Times*, for misuse of the term, with captions 'NOT THIS', 'NOT THIS', 'NOT EVEN THIS' and 'NOR THIS' beneath various solecisms.

These animals, it turns out, were probably known as Alderneys because all Channel Island cattle, whether transported for sale from Jersey, Guernsey, Alderney or France, arrived in England from the last port of call – Alderney – in what was known in the ports as the Alderney Boat. Only four per cent (or less) of cattle known as 'Alderneys' in the 18th and 19th centuries were from Alderney. All Channel Island and some French cattle were so similar that English buyers did not distinguish between them.

Guernsey and Jersey had banned each other's cattle from their shows by 1862, but there was free exchange between Guernsey and Alderney. When Alderney's forts were being built in the 1850s and 1860s, the island could not supply enough milk for all the extra workmen. So it imported more cattle from Guernsey. This led to cross-breeding of a new 'Alderney', which became famous for its beautiful udders and rich milk. However, Alderney cows were registered in 1910 as Guernseys, in order to sell them to Guernsey and then on, for large sums of money, to US farmers – who were only interested in cows if they were 'Guernseys'. The display bemoaned the situation: 'The prosperity of Alderney depended on the sale of these cattle to Guernsey.'

From 1927 all were crossbreeds. Between the evacuation of 1940, and the Germans' arrival, Guernsey farmers managed to rescue some of the cows and heifers. They were replaced on Alderney in 1945 – by Guernseys. According to the display, at the time of evacuation, 'many [bulls and cows] followed their owners and stood along the quay as the boats departed'. The museum display was completed, as a final tribute to 'our beautiful cows', with a large cabinet of trophies from cattle shows.

The story of the Alderney Cow has it all: inter-island rivalry, Nazis, war and money. I can imagine an American film producer holidaying on Alderney, looking at this display and dreaming up his next feature: *When Cows Came Home*.

***

But, for all the attractions and intrigue on the island, I was there for one main reason. It was time to meet Elisabeth Beresford.

I checked the pockets of my smart blue blazer and slipped the backpack over it, as I turned left out of the guesthouse for the cobbles of Victoria Street. No crowds would delay me – this was the main street of the island capital and I was the only pedestrian.

I paused at the bookshop. The owner was sitting at a smart mahogany desk talking into a telephone, with two dogs and a puppy curled up around his legs and the bottom of bookcases.

'Please don't let the puppy out,' said a sign on the door. I was the only customer I saw in the shop all week. Further down the hill, I admired the exterior of Riduna, a department store which had closed the previous year. The bottle blonde serving tea in the café opposite had told me that someone had bought the building; but nobody on Alderney knew who.

'It's extraordinary,' she said. 'Everybody knows everybody's business, but not this time.'

The exterior had looked like a complete mess until someone asked a local student to brighten it up. The result was a montage of Banksy-style pop art. One image showed a cat using a heavy drill; the caption was 'GOTTA GET OUT OF THIS PLACE'. A chimpanzee wore a placard with the warning 'LAUGH NOW, BUT ONE DAY WE'LL BE IN CHARGE'. A young man in a beanie hat brandished a begging bowl and declaimed 'KEEP YOUR COINS, I WANT CHANGE'. It was a refreshing, spiky antidote to the picture postcard prettiness of the rest of the street.

I chuckled again at the chalkboard advertisement outside the Rose and Crown:

'Husband crèche. Is he getting under your feet? Leave him here while you shop. Free crèche, we only charge for the drinks.'

The blue-facaded grocery Arkwright et Fils proclaimed that it was '*Ne pas ouvrir toutes heures*' (not open all hours), unlike the TV series which had inspired its name. I had gone in two days before; much to my disappointment, there was no owner with a stammer, the till didn't try to bite its operator and there was no buxom nurse in evidence (though there was a small nun buying washing-up liquid).

Alderney encourages you to take things slow. One shop is devoted to the sale of clocks which add '-ish' to every hour. I was so –ish on this particular day that I could have missed my appointment at the florist without a late, frenzied trot down the street. The shop was still shut for lunch but, a few minutes later, the shop assistant cycled up.

'Sorry I'm late,' she said. 'I was having a swim and the water was so lovely it seemed a crime to get out.'

I collected the arrangement of freesias I had ordered, and carried them in one hand, and headed down a

An echo of a famous TV series – a shop on Alderney

footpath towards the beach looking very smart. I might have been an odd sight, if anyone had been around to see it. If I had been wearing a tie, I'd have been straightening it all the way.

*** *

The door was unremarkable, plain and white, like the room into which I edged with my backpack, blazer, freesias and questions. A small, neat figure with short, straight grey hair sat by a desk. She was reading a hardback book.

'Hello,' I said. 'I've come to talk to you about the Wombles…'

She looked up and turned her gaze on me.

'*Have* you?'

'Well, yes… we arranged it a while ago…'

Had she forgotten? Her eyes alighted on the freesias.

'Those look jolly good. You'd better put them over here.'

I shuffled over to the desk, placing the flowers under

the unblinking gaze of Great Uncle Bulgaria, who was perched on top of more books. From the backpack, I took Bungo and placed him next to the books. I didn't have a business card, so Bungo was the next best thing in terms of credentials. Outside, someone was mowing a lawn. I looked out of a window at the sea. Waves were lapping at the empty beach under a cloudless sky.

'Of course you probably know that Ivor Wood was asked by FilmFair to design the puppets – he really was a very lugubrious sort of chap, I liked him very much, got on with him very well...'

No need to worry about where to begin; Mrs Beresford was off and talking, in a clear, firm, well-educated voice. Or should that be Elisabeth? Or Liza, as everyone seemed to call her? I settled for Liza.

'... I had to rush him into the nearest wine bar and get him a glass of wine and he used to utter "Oh, Liza" in tones of utter despondency... even when the BBC said "Yes, that's exactly what a Womble should look like". He started his own company later.'

Indeed he did, and it created *Postman Pat*.

'You know a lot more about children's television than I do!'

Was it true that Liza thought of the Wombles on Wimbledon Common?

'I had my lovely parents-in-law and mother-in-law's cousins staying over Christmas. All through Christmas Day I kept saying to Kate and Marcus, "Quiet, Grandfather's got a headache," or "Quiet, Gran-Gran's having a nap". On Boxing Day I turfed the children out of the car on Wimbledon Common near the Windmill; luckily it was deserted, I think it was a Sunday. I said to them: "Let it all go". So we ran backwards and forwards, screaming and shouting at the tops of our voices. Katie came back and said "Isn't it great on Wombledon Common". And I said, "That's where the Wombles live." And I went home and started writing it.'

The small hardback book was back on the desk now; her memories had her full attention. She reflected on her choice of place names for individual Wombles. Liza had based Orinoco on her son Marcus, but why Orinoco?

'I flew over the Orinoco river once. Which country is that in? Remind me.'

'Venezuela, in the north of South America.'

She looked hard at me, as if wondering whether this answer was reliable.

'Marcus was only a very small boy then. He's a very successful businessman now, a millionaire, running steam train trips round the UK. Prince Charles is a big fan, you know.'

Liza's daughter Kate had gone to Cholet on a school exchange trip, and Madame Cholet was based on Liza's mother – 'a wonderful cook'. A nephew went to Wellington School in Somerset, hence Wellington.

'Tobermory was based on my favourite brother, who was 10 years older than me - and a wonderful brother. He used to work for Sir Robert Watson-Watt, the man who started radar. When my brother retired, he and his wife packed up their things and went to live in Tobermory. I've always thought it was to get away from his mother, who adored him!'

Which left...

'Tomsk was based on my husband Max [Robertson]'s goddaughter Eleanor Craxton. Great Uncle Bulgaria was inspired by my father-in-law. He was wonderful, very good to me. Bungo was based on Kate – because she's a bit bossy!'

But what were the connections with the place names?

'Oh, none at all, dear heart. I picked them out of Katie's school atlas.'

I felt a stab of irrational disappointment. I'd wondered why Liza had chosen Bungo, as it was no longer in use in Japan, but there was no reason. On the other hand, here was a case of life and art imitating each other. Each Womble chose his or her name from Great Uncle Bulgaria's atlas. So why shouldn't Liza do the same? I asked about how life changed after the Wombles became media megastars.

'The first Wombles books sold quite well. But after the first TV series went out, I was deluged – everybody was after me. The manufacturers too – you could buy Wombles clothes, decorations, everything. The country went Wombles-mad.'

Over 35 years after the event, she still sounded astonished.

'The money from the Wombles started me off as a foster parent to children in the Third World. I still have foster children. I also started the first private school Alderney ever had, as a trustee. Max said I had to come somewhere they paid low tax – that's why we came to Alderney. I didn't want to leave England at all – I didn't like leaving the family behind.'

Families, and their quirks, were one of Liza's recurring topics of conversation.

'I had a bit of a tough life when I was a girl – my mother just didn't like girls – I had three older brothers. One changed his name to Mark Brandel and ended up as a screenwriter in Hollywood. He ran away with one of the Mitford sisters while he was still at school. It was kept from me as I was very much the youngest sister – my brothers were 12, ten and eight years older than me. I was the most unimportant person in the family, simple as that. What a family, eh? My father [JD Beresford] was a very highbrow writer. I don't think he'd be very proud of me. Nobody ever called me that – but I'm a bookaholic – a passionate reader.'

These last comments had an inescapable wistful note. I could have said that of course he would be proud of her; I thought of saying that the world knew about the Wombles, but not many people these days had heard of JD Beresford. I said nothing, preferring to read a printout from an online biography of JD which Liza had passed to me. JD had run off with another woman, leaving Liza's mother alone.

'I wrote a lot of other children's books, many of them before the Wombles. There was a whole series of books about magic. We needed the money – I had to support my mother. You've never seen anyone work as hard as I did.'

I looked at the book Liza had been reading when I came in. Its title was *Saturday's Child*.

'That's one of my romantic novels. I wrote quite a lot of them – thirteen so far. *Saturday's Child* is my favourite; that's why I'm re-reading it at the moment. The romantic novels often happened while Max and I were travelling for work.'

I had known about the other children's books, but not the romantic novels. Just how many books had Liza written? The question surprised her.

'I don't know – I never kept an account. Can't remember half the stuff I wrote. I only write a diary now. You can't live without writing in a way. It settles a lot of arguments!'

Liza had been a journalist and broadcaster for a number of years before the Wombles came along. She worked at the Central Office of Information for 'a lovely man called Con Ryan who taught me how to write'. One of the assignments on which he sent a young Liza was to interview the Duke of Bedford...

'The Duke was opening his rather palatial room to the public to raise money. I was getting on very well, he was very nice and then his second wife came back unexpectedly early. She saw us together and started to chase us from room to room saying "Who is that woman?" We finished the interview with the Duke carrying the recorder and me carrying the mic, running from room to room...

'I remember having to go to interview Mrs Thatcher. It was like interviewing royalty, she was surrounded by lots of very pretty ladies-in-waiting. You ended up doing some very strange jobs! Then the world went Womble-mad...'

The madness included a MBE for Liza – and contrasting receptions from two royals.

'I was presented to the Duke of Edinburgh, who said: "Why did you leave Wimbledon?" I said, "Sir, we never lived there, we lived in Wandsworth." He said "Wandsworth?", turned on his heel and never spoke to me again!

'My oldest brother Tristram worked for the Duke of Edinburgh at Buckingham Palace and I can remember him saying that nobody realised how hard the Duke worked. He got a CBE for services to agriculture. My mother loved royalty and tried to get information out of Tristram but, of course, he was incredibly discreet.

'The Queen was a fan. I went to Buckingham Palace for the investiture and I took Kate and Marcus and a young friend of the family. I was terrified the whole time I was in there. She knew more about the Wombles than I did. I think it was a relief for her when I finally got out and joined the others. Marcus said "Ma, I've timed you. The Queen spent longer with you than anyone else and I think MBE stands for Mother's Best Efforts." Ever since then, it's been known as Mother's Best Efforts. Kate is the only person who ever uses the MBE – she puts it on the envelope when she writes to me.'

Liza seemed to enjoy being well-connected. Walter de la Mare was Tristram's godfather and wrote a poem dedicated to Liza, while her godmother was Eleanor Farjeon, a children's writer and poet. But I wondered how she valued the money she had made, and the recognition she had gained, in the balance against her parents' love and approval.

'My mother was in her late 40s when I was born. She never made any secret of the fact she didn't like women, she certainly didn't want a daughter – how I managed to grow up as normal as I did, I don't know. By the time the Wombles furore started, she was in a home. She used to insist on having "her" Wombles all the way round the bed. Just before she died, she said: "Elisabeth, I never loved you, I never wanted you, but I have to admit you turned out the best of all my children."'

Later that day, I walked past a certain house and looked at the windows. On the sills were the unmistakable figures of Wombles; some small versions on the upper window sills, as sold by McDonald's in the 1990s, and larger toys, including another Great Uncle Bulgaria, on the lower sills.

'Well,' said Liza, summing up, 'The Wombles made people laugh. That was the main thing.'

They did more than that, I said. They were early symbols of environmentalism.

'That's right, they were. I used to hate all that rubbish lying around.'

I told Liza about Gail, and Clive, and the Orinoco store; all of whom were following the Wombles' example in their own ways.

'Good God,' was all she could say in reply.

I put my notebook away and got ready to leave.

'Goodbye, Bulgaria,' I said to the toy on top of the books on the desk.

'*Great Uncle* Bulgaria,' Liza corrected me. I like to think there was a twinkle in her eye.

Later, the island shrank below us as the plane started its return journey. This time I had two window seats, as nobody had booked the seat next to me, so Bungo and the backpack were there. Charles had told me that the occasional visitor booked plane seats for his or her dog. I don't know if he made that up, but 45 minutes of sitting next to (say) a St Bernard might have been interesting.

As we travelled from island to mainland, I thought of Elisabeth Beresford, whose clear eyes, vivid imagination and hard work had created the Wombles. If she had had a different childhood, would she have done all that? Or was she a little like Alderney itself – spurred on by lack of attention to work harder than the rest? *Saturday's child works hard for a living.*

* * *

And now Orinoco is back in the green leather chair, gazing out at an English spring day. Now he has three other Wombles for company: Great Uncle Bulgaria, Bungo and Wellington. The chair is big enough for the four of them; there's no bickering.

The Wombles may not travel so much from now on, but they're busy. The original books have been republished, the original albums re-released and the Wombles even performed at Glastonbury. Good thing they weren't on the same stage as The Wombats; imagine the confusion…

My quest has come to an end – although there are plenty more places I could visit in future which gave their names to Wombles. The Cairngorms… Adelaide… I wouldn't mind going back to Japan to see Tokyo. The other Wellingtons around the world could keep me travelling for months.

But it's been a great experience, visiting Orinoco and Tobermory and Bulgaria and Tomsk and Cholet and Wellington (two of them) and Shansi and Bungo and Alderney. Each place has had its charms, its surprises and an inner Womble-ness. I'd be more than happy to revisit them all.

Then there were the people I met, some of them taking direct inspiration from the Wombles, others living and working in ways of which our friendly furry Wimbledon burrow-dwellers would approve: Clive changing the face of Sussex with his guerrilla gardening, Gail researching ways to live in a sustainable manner, Kato in Kitakyushu evangelising for the use of eco-homes. In an age of supposed globalisation, it was heartening to see how big, and strange, and mad and diverse our world is; and how proud so many people were of their home towns, whether it was Harry in Wellington, Shropshire, or Natasha in Tomsk.

And there were the sights I saw, and the things I was able to do. Without the Wombles, I wouldn't have gone piranha fishing, or tried deep fried Mars bars or bracken jelly, or gone to Hell (I forgive them for that one), or travelled on the Trans-Siberian Express and the Japanese bullet trains, or visited an English pub in Siberia, or danced with a donkey in France. I wouldn't have learned a little about all the places, and I wouldn't be taking extra interest whenever I see any of them on the news, or read about them in the newspapers. The old saying is true. Travel with Wombles broadens the mind.

All this because of a Boxing Day walk on a common and a little girl's slip of the tongue, and a clever, energetic, imaginative writer who created an unforgettable set of characters. I wonder if Elisabeth Beresford knew how many people loved the Wombles, and how many people's lives would be so different without them.

Thanks, Liza.